PALESTINE IMMIGRATION POLICY
UNDER SIR HERBERT SAMUEL

Palestine Immigration Policy
under
Sir Herbert Samuel

British, Zionist and Arab
Attitudes

M. Mossek

FRANK CASS

First published 1978 in Great Britain by
FRANK CASS AND COMPANY LIMITED
Gainsborough House, Gainsborough Road,
London E11 1RS, England

and in the United States of America by
FRANK CASS AND COMPANY LIMITED
c/o Biblio Distribution Centre,
81 Adams Drive, P.O. Box 327, Totowa, N.J. 07511

British Library Cataloguing in Publication Data
Mossek, M
    Palestine immigration policy under Sir Herbert Samuel.
    1. Israel — Emigration and immigration
    I. Title
    325.5694   JV8749.1/

ISBN 0-7146-3096-9

Printed in Great Britain by
Billing & Sons Ltd, Guildford, London and Worcester

To Mirel

CONTENTS

Preface ix

Abbreviations xii

Chapter 1 PRIMARY FORMATION OF IMMIGRATION POLICY 1

Samuel's Route to Jerusalem 1

Outlining of the Policy 4

The First Immigration Ordinance 6

Forming of the Department of Immigration and Travel 7

Implementation of the Policy 8

Attempts to Restrict Immigration 11

Chapter 2 THE TURNING POINT — TEMPORARY SUSPENSION OF IMMIGRATION 17

The Palestine Phase 17

The London Phase 24

Morris's Mission — The Continent Phase 28

Chapter 3 REVIEW OF IMMIGRATION POLICY: THE ROAD TO THE WHITE PAPER 35

Outlining of New Schemes of Control 35

Zionist Campaign in London: Efforts to Turn Back the Clock 40

Towards a Working Agreement 51

Chapter 4 THE NEW POLICY: ZIONIST AND ARAB REACTION 65

Co-operation or Non-Co-operation: the Dilemma of the Palestine Zionist Executive 65

Arab Rejection of the Constitutional Proposals 71

Chapter 5   **REORGANISATION OF THE**
DEPARTMENT OF IMMIGRATION
AND TRAVEL: ATTEMPTS TO
ADJUST ITS MACHINERY TO THE
NEW SCHEME OF CONTROL   **82**
    The Tendency Towards Extension   82
    The Tendency Towards Reduction   86

Chapter 6   **THE IMMIGRATION ORDINANCE,**
1925   **95**
    The Campaign over the Immigration
    Scheme   95
    Legislation of the Ordinance   108

Chapter 7   **EBB AND FLOW: ECONOMIC**
ABSORPTIVE CAPACITY AS A
CRITERION FOR IMMIGRATION   **117**
    Inauguration of the New Policy   117
    Operation of the Labour Schedule   121
    Immigration under Category "D":
    the Case of The Fiancées   133
    Middle Class Immigration   138

Conclusion   152

Appendices   157

Bibliography   172

Index   177

PREFACE

Among the numerous historical works on Mandatory Palestine, studies dealing with policy-making are relatively scarce in comparison with those dealing with general political questions. Until recent years, various economic questions, land settlement, colonization, immigration, education, social welfare policy, etc. have not had much profound or exhaustive research devoted to them. Although these topics were dealt with in British official publications in the form of reports and surveys, they generally go no further than descriptions of the facts and events, without analysing the concepts, motives or contributions of the bodies and individuals who took part in outlining the policy. On the other hand, memoirs, monographs and general books wholly or partly dealing with these subjects usually have a rather tendentious approach which spotlights the political aspects of the problem or emphasises the different viewpoints of their authors. A serious obstacle which stood in the way of researchers until recent years was the unavailability of archival material which is indispensable to studies of policy-making.

The recent opening to the public of archival material of the period concerned has made possible direct access to the official files of the bodies which participated in, or had an influence upon the making of immigration policy. The five principal bodies concerned were the Palestine Administration, the Colonial Office, the Foreign Office, the Zionist Executive in London and the Palestine Zionist Executive.

The material of the Palestine Administration is kept in the Israel State Archives (I.S.A.), in Jerusalem. The relevant material mainly includes the files of the Immigration Department, the Chief Secretary and correspondence between the High Commissioner and the Colonial Office. The latter correspondence, and in addition, internal minutes and memoranda of the Colonial Office are also kept in London, at the Public Record Office (P.R.O.). Also available at the Public Record Office is the correspondence between the Colonial Office and the Foreign Office and the Foreign Office with the British Consuls, regarding control of immigration.

Zionist material is concentrated in the Central Zionist Archives (C.Z.A.), in Jerusalem. This material includes correspondence of the Palestine Zionist Executive with the Palestine Administration and the Zionist Executive in London, as well as correspondence between the latter body and the Colonial and the Foreign Office. Particularly important are the confidential Minutes of the Zionist Executive and the Palestine Zionist Executive, which were both closed until recent years.

Complementary to the Zionist material are the private papers of Chaim Weizmann, the President of the Zionist Organisation during the period concerned, which are kept at the Weizmann Memorial in Rehovot, Israel.

When referring to archival sources I have given full details of the documents in the following order: sender, addressee, number and date and then, archival group, serial number, volume, file and paper. Most of the material is in English. Translations of quotations from Hebrew are my own and from Arabic according to the official English translations as they appear in the files.

I have supplemented the archival material with official publications of the Palestine and British Governments and the Zionist Organisation. The particular importance of these sources is their ability to reflect the official policy in the form of statements, laws and statistical data. In most cases I preferred the reliability of archival material to the official publications.

Although memoirs and biographies have provided me with much fascinating historical material, these are sometimes of limited reliability. Nevertheless, I was able to make use of diaries, in particular those of Colonel Kisch and Dr. Ruppin of the Palestine Zionist Executive.

The contribution of general books and monographs to my study is not very significant as most of them seem to have been based exclusively on official publications. However, doctoral theses written in recent years on various Palestine questions have been of great assistance to me.

Published material is referred to in the footnotes by the author's name and title in brief. Full details of these sources may be found in the bibliographical list.

Finally, I wish to express my thanks to the Director and staff of the Public Record Office for their kind permission to consult material and for their help; to Dr. M. Heimann and Mr. I. Philip of the Central Zionist Archives, Jerusalem; to Mr. Julian L. Meltzer and Mrs. L. Calef of the Weizmann Archives, Rehovot; to Mr. H. Solomon and Miss Y. Teslitski, my colleagues at the Israel State Archives and particularly to Dr. P. A. Alsberg, the Israel State Archivist.

I was fortunate to have had the guidance and encouragement of Professor Elie Kedourie, to whom I owe special thanks. I am also most grateful to my good friends Dr. Neil Caplan and Mr. Chaim Baram, who took the trouble to go through this study and gave me a great deal of sound advice. And most of all, to my wife, Marlene, without whose patience and constant support this work would not have been completed.

This research was made possible by the generous support of the following bodies:— The Jewish Agency, Jerusalem; the Jewish Memorial Council, New York; The B'nai B'rith and Anglo-Jewish Association, London; and the Central Research Fund of the University of London.

JERUSALEM   M.M.

ABBREVIATIONS

AE	Arab Executive; Executive Committee of Palestine Arab Congress
CO	Colonial Office
CS	Chief (Civil) Secretary, Palestine Government
CZA	Central Zionist Archives
CZO	Central Zionist Office, London
DIT	Department of Immigration and Travel, Palestine Government
FO	Foreign Office
HC	High Commissioner of Palestine
HO	Home Office
ISA	Israel State Archives
PRO	Public Record Office
PZE	Palestine Zionist Executive
VLE	Va'ad Leumi (Executive)
WA	Weizmann Archives
ZC	Zionist Commission to Palestine
ZE	Zionist Executive, London
ZO	Zionist Organisation

Chapter One

PRIMARY FORMATION OF
IMMIGRATION POLICY

SAMUEL'S ROUTE TO JERUSALEM

On the morning of April 24th 1920, one day before the Allied Powers at the San Remo Peace Conference assigned the mandate over Palestine to Great Britain, the heads of the British Delegation to the Conference — Prime Minister Lloyd George and Foreign Secretary Lord Curzon — decided to end the Military Administration in Palestine and to appoint Herbert Samuel head of the new Civil Administration.[1] The political implications of this decision were of crucial importance, in particular to the Zionist cause: Palestine was assigned de facto to Britain, without waiting for the Peace Treaty to be signed with Turkey and before the Mandate was approved by the League of Nations; the country was transferred from the supervision of the G.H.Q. in Cairo and the War Office to the Eastern Department of the Foreign Office, which tended to show more sympathy with Zionism; martial law was to be abolished and with it the necessity of keeping to the status quo ante bellum, which was used by the Military Administration to justify the curbing of the Zionist enterprise in Palestine. Thus, some of the legal and political obstacles in the way of the building up of the Jewish National Home were formally removed.

Not less significant was the decision to appoint Herbert Samuel as first High Commissioner to Palestine. Samuel,

1

one of the principal leaders of the Liberal Party, was the first professing Jew ever to sit in a British Cabinet, a fact which he greatly appreciated, being proud of his origin. Although he testified in his memoirs that he had taken no special interest in the idea of Jewish nationalism until the First World War, as any practical outcome of Zionism seemed to him 'remote',[2] at his first meeting with Weizmann in December 1914, he admitted that 'he was not a stranger to Zionist ideas; he had been following them up a little of late years and although he had never mentioned it, he took a considerable interest in the question'.[3]

At any rate, Britain's declaration of war on Turkey in November 1914, and with it, her intention of destroying the Ottoman Empire, immediately spurred Samuel on to open Zionist activity.

It would seem that these events gave Samuel a suitable opportunity of releasing his hitherto latent sympathy towards Jewish nationalism, since he became an active Zionist without external pressures and before he had met any Zionist leaders. Convinced of the great and variegated talents of the Jewish 'race' and of the contribution that a Jewish State in Palestine would make to the strategic interests of the British Empire, Samuel began, as early as November 1914, to recruit supporters of his idea from among his colleagues in the Cabinet. His main efforts were focused upon convincing the Prime Minister, Herbert Asquith and the Foreign Secretary, Edward Grey, to accept his plan.[4] Later on, after he had met Zionist leaders and learned of the poor conditions in Palestine and the limited abilities of the Zionist movement at that time, he withdrew his radical plan for a Jewish State and suggested establishing a British protectorate over Palestine where 'under British rule, facilities would be given to Jewish organisations to purchase land, to found colonies, to establish educational and religious institutions, and to co-operate in the economic development of the country, and that Jewish immigration, carefully regulated, would be given preference, so that in the course of time the Jewish inhabitants, grown into a majority and settled in the land, may be conceded such degree of self-government as the conditions of that day might justify'.[5]

Samuel failed to gain any substantial support from his colleagues for his proposals. The British Zionists, however, were understandably most enthusiastic. After his first interview with Samuel in December, Weizmann, deeply impressed by Samuel's ardent Zionist views, confessed: 'If I were a religious Jew I should have thought the Messianic times were near.'[6] Three months later he was able to consider Samuel his confidant, telling him of all recent developments and added, 'you were good enough to guide us up to now, and I am sure you will continue to help us. We look to you and to your historical role which you are playing and will play in the redemption of Israel'.[7]

Out of office from December 1916, Samuel continued to exert his still considerable influence in the same direction as before. In October 1917, when the fate of the Balfour Declaration was in balance, he was consulted by the War Cabinet and in his reply set out the case for the policy which he had consistently advocated for nearly three years. Though he was not a member of the Zionist Organisation in the years 1918 and 1919, he was closely co-operating with the Zionists and acting as their adviser on economic and political matters and as Chairman of internal committees of the Organisation. In fulfilling these roles, he acted with the co-operation and the confidence of both the Zionist Organisation and the British Government. By virtue of this confidence and his personal qualities and experience, he was sent by the Foreign Office to Palestine in December 1919 to report upon 'financial and administrative conditions there, and to advise concerning the line of policy to be followed in future in these respects, should the mandate fall to Great Britain'.[8]

During this entire period the Zionists did not conceal their desire to see Samuel as the head of the future Civil Administration of Palestine.[9] The fact that he was an avowed Zionist not only did not disqualify him in the eyes of the British, but added to his credit. 'It is essential', the Prime Minister told Samuel in San Remo, when offering him the post in Palestine, 'to have someone who is interested in making the policy a success'.[10] Samuel, however, had serious doubts concerning the political wisdom of appointing a Jew for such a delicate post. Although he believed that he could be 'useful' and being deeply interested in the Zionist idea he would be willing 'to make any sacrifice to promote its success', he revealed his fears to the Prime Minister that 'such an appointment was open to the danger that measures, which the non-Jewish population would accept from a British Christian Governor, might be objected to if adopted by a Jew'.[11] Nevertheless, the next day, following long discussions with the Zionist leaders, who exerted great pressure on him to take up the post, he wrote to the Prime Minister, accepting the offer. In his letter, he substantiates his consent with the additional advantage to the fulfilment of the Zionist programme, which must, 'from the nature of the case, be gradual and very considerate for the interests of the Arabs and Christians'. 'Jewry in Palestine and throughout the world', he wrote, 'would be more likely to practise patience, without losing enthusiasm, if the pace were set by an Administrator who was known to be in full sympathy with the ultimate aim, than if it were set by anyone else . . .'[12]

Samuel's reasons in both directions for rejecting the post and for accepting it epitomise the problems of his future five year rule in Palestine.

OUTLINING OF THE POLICY

From San Remo, Samuel hastened to London for consultations. The formulation of immigration policy became one of the main issues of his intensive discussions with the Foreign Office and the Zionist Executive in London. Samuel chose to meet first with the Zionists in order to learn their demands and to formulate accordingly the policy he intended to present to the Government.

On 4th June, he met Dr. Weizmann, Nahum Sokolow and other representatives of the Zionist Organisation. The Zionist leaders put forward three main principles which, according to them were vital for constructive implementation of immigration policy: first, that the entry of Jews into Palestine should be facilitated; second, there should be no 'organised immigration' into Palestine unless with the consent of the Zionist Organisation; third, that the Zionist Organisation would be authorised to permit entry to

Palestine of all Jews if in its opinion they had 'independent means of subsistence or a reasonably assured opportunity of sustaining themselves by their own labour'.[13] Samuel accepted the Zionist demands in principle and suggested establishing half yearly schedules for labour immigration to those to whom the Zionist Organisation could guarantee a livelihood for one year. In this manner, he believed, the Zionist Organisation would be authorised to select Jewish immigration according to their own discretion and to prevent the entry of undesirable elements from an economic or political point of view. In his opinion, this could also contradict any claims from 'opponents to Zionism', that the Zionists were bringing in a mass of destitute refugees who would be a burden on the inhabitants of the country. Samuel pointed out, and Dr. Weizmann agreed, that the Zionists' guarantee was also necessary to strengthen the hands of the Organisation itself in refusing applications of those who, in its judgement, would not be able to find employment in the country.

Thus both Samuel and the Zionists were unanimous in their opposition to 'free immigration', at least 'for a gradual transition period of a few years'. Nevertheless, Samuel gave his word that Jews would have preference over non-Jews by their exclusive right to apply to the Zionist Organisation for permits. 'In practice', he promised, 'the Zionists would get what they wanted by their right of franking any number of immigrants so long as they were capable of being sustained in Palestine.'

A further Zionist demand to set up a Joint Immigration Board of equal representation of the Administration and the Zionist Organisation, was rejected by Samuel as unwise from a political point of view, since if such a board were established other political interests such as the Palestinian Arabs would ask for similar representation. Samuel assured the Zionists that their interests 'would be equally well served by informal consultation'.

On the basis of the Zionist demands and the agreement reached with them, Samuel presented a memorandum containing his own proposals for control of immigration into Palestine to the Foreign Office. His proposals were based on the assumptions that 'it is essential to make a beginning as soon as possible with the establishment of the Jewish National Home', that there is a 'considerable demand for various kinds of labour in Palestine' and if immigration were not permitted 'the economic development of the country will be retarded'. According to his scheme, the Zionist Organisation would be asked to present half-yearly labour schedules which would be checked by the Palestine Administration, who would ultimately decide the numbers. The Organisation would be authorised to issue recommendations to the British Consuls up to that number; the Consuls would be instructed to accept those recommendations and to issue visas 'in every case unless there was a definite reason to the contrary'. Other people (Jews or non-Jews) might apply to the Consuls who would be instructed to give visas to such persons as they considered to be self-supporting or could find employment in Palestine.[14]

Samuel's proposals, after being approved by the Foreign Office,[15] outlined the general nature of the first Palestine Immigration Ordinance and the first Instructions (of the Foreign Office) to His Majesty's Consuls.

THE FIRST IMMIGRATION ORDINANCE

When Civil Administration was set up in Palestine, first priority was given to the drafting of the Immigration Ordinance,[16] in order to fill in a void left by the abolition of the military permits system.[17] The political importance of the entire question obliged the Legal Department, when drafting the Ordinance, to co-operate with the Civil Secretary (later known as Chief Secretary) and with the High Commissioner himself. This work was facilitated by the fact that an ardent Zionist, Norman Bentwich, stood at the head of the Legal Department. In fact, Bentwich was inclined to favour the Zionist demands in order to facilitate immigration into Palestine.[18]

The drafting of the Ordinance was accompanied by frequent consultations with the Zionist Commission, the local representation of the Zionist Organisation in Palestine. Dr. Eder, the Political Secretary of the Commission who presented its reservations on the draft Ordinance, suggested only the inclusion of a list of illnesses, sufferers from which would not be permitted entry to Palestine, and that persons who had obtained Palestinian citizenship, although five years had not elapsed since their entry to Palestine, should not be expelled. These two reservations were accepted. An additional request for the right to appeal of anyone expelled was rejected.[19] The trivial nature of these amendments pointed to the Zionists' general satisfaction with the draft.

Simultaneously with the drafting of the Ordinance in Jerusalem an Inter-Departmental Committee in London was at work. The participants of this Committee were representatives of the Eastern and Passport Control Departments of the Foreign Office and representatives of the Home Office, who were invited to advise the Committee on outlining an immigration policy. The extensive representation in the Committee testifies to the importance which the Foreign Office attached to the question. The final draft of the Ordinance, as drafted in Jerusalem, was discussed by the Committee, which suggested a few minor amendments to prevent possible misunderstandings or loopholes in the law.[20] Following approval of the Foreign Office, the Ordinance was published in Palestine and enforced as from 1st September 1920.[21]

In general, one may say that the Ordinance was extremely liberal, permitting immigration to anyone who was healthy in body and mind and assured of a livelihood, provided he did not pose any political or criminal danger to society.

FORMING OF THE DEPARTMENT OF IMMIGRATION AND TRAVEL

To carry out immigration policy, Samuel set up an Immigration and Travel Department. In the formal hierarchy of the Administration, the new department was a lesser one and belonged to the group of minor departments, together with the Department of Ports and Land Registration.[22] This inferiority was rather semantic; however the exclusion of the Director of the Immigration Department from the Palestine Advisory Council was significant. Members of this body included, as well as District Governors, a considerable number of heads of Department, among them even the Directors of the Post and Telegraph and Public Works.[23]

This was rather surprising considering the great importance which Samuel attached to the immigration question. It appears that he wished to play down the whole question of immigration intentionally and to limit the tasks of the Department to control of immigration only, by leaving policy-making to himself and his senior officials, while unofficially consulting the Zionists, as he had promised them at the meeting of 4th June.[24]

In accordance with its functions, the Department's budget was reduced to less than 1% of the Administration's total budget.[25] The Department's expenses were designed to be met by revenues coming from registration and landing fees.[26] Any claims that the Department's expenses were a burden on the Palestinian taxpayer could thus be disproved.[27]

A certain bias was apparent in choosing senior staff for the Department. The fact that three out of the five senior officials were British Jews stood out: N. I. Mindel, the Immigration Officer in Jaffa, the main port of immigration; Dennis Cohen, the Immigration Officer in Jerusalem; and Albert Hyamson, the Assistant Director of the Department. Hyamson, one of the central activists of the Zionist movement in Great Britain and a member of Weizmann's 'inner circle' during the First World War,[28] was brought especially for this post. Major Morris, Director of the Department, was posted as a temporary member of the establishment, whereas Hyamson was offered permanent employment from the outset.[29] Several years later this fact became a pretext for removing Morris from the Directorship and appointing Hyamson in his place.[30]

IMPLEMENTATION OF THE POLICY

'The San Remo Resolution', a brilliant diplomatic achievement for the Zionists, presented the greatest practical challenge they had ever had — the building up of the Jewish National Home. Yet the joy of victory was clouded by doubts concerning their limited abilities. 'The fate of all Zionism depends on this', wrote Weizmann prior to the

Resolution, 'since when the mandate is handed over to England, it will be necessary to make immediate arrangements for immigration to Palestine, and in order to begin this, we need £1 million sterling at least. Only the Americans can produce such a sum, and if this amount is not collected, then we shall be in trouble. England will see the Jews as fanciful, and not to be taken seriously, i.e. the end of all our hopes.'[31]

These hopes were far from being fulfilled. At the Zionist Conference held in London in July 1920 controversy broke out between the 'American group', headed by Justice Brandeis, and the 'European group', headed by Weizmann, concerning the Organisation's budget. Weizmann set this at something in the neighbourhood of £2 million a year, assuming that the major part of the sum would come from American Jewry. The Americans, shocked by this 'astronomical figure', could not guarantee more than £100,000.[32] This state of affairs more than anything else determined Zionist immigration policy for the coming decade.

Nevertheless, both the enthusiasm of the Zionist movement after San Remo and the appointment of Herbert Samuel as 'first High Commissioner for Judea' encouraged the Zionist leadership to initiate a daring and large-scale policy on immigration. It will be remembered that Samuel proposed permitting the Zionists to admit a set number of immigrants, who were certain of obtaining employment and a living. This schedule had already been considered at Samuel's first meeting with the Zionist Commission. Dr. Ruppin, the economic expert of the Commission, suggested that the schedule for the first year should allow up to 10,000 working immigrants, to be employed in forestry (5,000), building (3,000), and roads (2,000).[34] Later on, the Zionist Commission presented a more enlarged and detailed programme which raised the number of working immigrants to 17,000.[35] The schedule was generally approved by the Government and fixed at 16,500 for the first year. It was also agreed that those immigrants could be accompanied by their families, i.e. wife and children under 16 and persons wholly dependent upon them, but for the purposes of the schedule members of the family would not count.[36] The number of labour immigrants including their families was likely to reach 70,000, thus doubling the Jewish community in Palestine in the course of one year.

Encouraging reports of great enthusiasm for immigration to Palestine, from Zionist Offices in Europe, assured the Zionists that they could easily fulfil the proposed schedule. Furthermore, Samuel agreed to a request from the Zionist Commission that all immigrants who had been detained in Europe and neighbouring countries of Palestine during the Military Administration should be allowed to enter without restrictions before the enforcement of the Immigration Ordinance.[37] This liberal policy — which continued also after the Ordinance became valid on 1st September 1920 — brought 4,000 immigrants to Palestine by the end of October, almost all of them with the sanction of the Zionist Commission.[38]

Although these numbers were still far less than agreed in the schedule, the Zionist Commission very soon found itself in serious difficulties in providing employment and minimum means of subsistence for the new arrivals. These difficulties placed the Commission in a grave dilemma. On the one hand they did not dare to ask the Government to restrict immigration, apparently to avoid bringing their failure into the open and thus creating a dangerous precedent of restrictions. On the other hand, to leave the flow of immigration as it was, could only worsen the situation.[39] The most honourable way out was to report to the Zionist Executive in London and ask them to postpone labour immigration for a time. 'The present mode of immigration', stated a report from Palestine, 'means nothing less than an early collapse, an early emigration and the destruction of every possibility to create in the near future the conditions for a more orderly and more extensive immigration.'[40] Yet the Zionist Executive, placed in the same dilemma, was neither in a hurry to spread the discouraging news from Palestine to its offices in Europe, nor was it in a position to admit its difficulties to the Foreign Office.

Samuel, doubtless well aware of the situation, also refrained from harming the Zionists' image at such an early stage. Convinced of the Zionists' ability to obtain the necessary funds for a constructive absorption of immigration and even to grant a development loan of £2.5 million to the Government for the same purpose,[41] he did not act instantly to restrict immigration. In his monthly reports to London he emphasised the flourishing economic future and the increasing numbers of immigrants with independent means.[42]

Immigration during the first six months of the new regime did not run strictly according to the immigration scheme as proposed by Samuel and approved by the Foreign Office. Large groups of immigrants, mostly young pioneers (Halutzim), gathered at the main ports and cities of Eastern Europe ready to leave for Palestine. On their behalf, local Zionist Offices pressed the British Consuls for visas and the Consuls requested instructions from London. The Foreign Office, 'extremely satisfied with the way events were shaping up in Palestine',[43] instructed its representatives in Europe to grant visas to immigrants recommended by the local branches of the Zionist Organisation.[44] It would appear that no one in Whitehall had paid serious attention to the fact that immigration under this category was limited numerically and that the British Consuls were not authorised to exceed the Immigration Schedule. In Bratislava, for instance, in a short space of time the British Consul franked 700 visas for immigrants recommended by the local Zionist Office.[45]

Samuel, aware of the danger of this procedure, cabled to London: 'it conflicts with policy approved by you of limitation of immigration according to economic capacity of the country to absorb immigrants and with arrangements with the Zionist Organisation for agreed schedules of immigrants and their responsible persons introduced by them', and urged that Consuls be instructed accordingly.[46] But Foreign Office officials interpreted this as if Samuel was intending to limit immigration only to immigrants recommended by the Zionist Organisation and would not agree to make any further changes.[47]

ATTEMPTS TO RESTRICT IMMIGRATION

After prolonged hesitations the Zionist Executive decided to reveal its difficulties to the Foreign Office. This delicate and rather unpleasant task fell to Leonard Stein, the young Acting Political Secretary of the Zionist Executive.

At an interview with R. T. Parkin of the Passport Control Department at the end of October, Stein revealed the financial difficulties of the Zionist Organisation in absorbing immigration and asked for the immigration schedule to be reduced from 16,500 as agreed, to 1,000. After indirectly accusing the British Consuls of exceeding their allocation, he urged that no further visas be granted to those recommended by the Zionist Offices until further notice.[48]

From this interview and further contacts with the Zionists, Foreign Office officials gathered that the Zionist Organisation was holding the Passport Control Officers and the Consuls responsible for lack of control, thus ridding themselves of any responsibility for these immigrants.[49] This feeling became more concrete after the Zionists requested that the words 'employment and accommodation in Palestine for a period of one year from the date of arrival' be deleted from their own written obligation to take care of recommended immigrants on the grounds 'that the words might be taken to imply some obligation by the Zionist Organisation towards the individual'.[50] A few days later, the Zionists declared unequivocally that 'no financial responsibility can be accepted by the Zionist Organisation in respect of immigrants who are not vouched for by the authorised Zionist Representatives'.[51]

Parallel to the Zionists' diplomatic attempts to restrict immigration by utilizing the Foreign Office machinery, the Central Zionist Office in London evolved a rigid and complex system of control in order to centralize supervision over its Offices and regulate immigration. The new system included: allotment of a limited number of Immigration Certificates to every Zionist Office and official recommendation forms to be supplied only by the Central Office. Specimens of both forms were sent through the Foreign Office to all British Consuls and Passport Control Officers, with the intention of avoiding forgeries and irregularities, either of individuals or of the Zionist Offices.[52] When this machinery was finally set up at the end of 1920 and the

Central Office issued the first 400 'authorised' certificates to its branches, over 5,000 'recommended' immigrants had already entered Palestine.[53] During the following months, the Central Office, in response to constant pressure from its branches, continued to allocate further certificates. By May 1921, 1,900 additional certificates had been issued by London, while over 3,000 'recommended' immigrants without authorised certificates entered Palestine.[54]

Simultaneously with the reorganisation of the Zionist immigration system, the Central Office launched a discreet publicity campaign with the intention of cooling down enthusiasm for immigration. In the first circular letter to its branches dated October 1920, the Zionist Executive chose to give details of instructions which the Foreign Office had issued to consuls in August. Nevertheless, it was brought to the attention of the Zionist branches that single immigrants would find employment conditions in Palestine more suitable than heads of families, since salaries for unskilled workers were low and for 'intelligent and professional workers there are no prospects of finding work in their profession'.[55] This was only a slight hint of the new policy to come. However, it seems that the Zionist Executive did not consider the circular to be up to date and decided to postpone its distribution. The next month's circular was sent out with an accompanying letter, revealing the agreement with the Foreign Office to reduce the certificates from 16,500 to 1,000 and that bachelors only would be accepted as immigrants.[56] The December circular letter, 'not for publication', instructed the Zionist representatives 'to draw the utmost attention of every immigrant to the present existing economic and sanitary conditions in Palestine, to the nature of labour, to the unsatisfactory housing conditions and wage situation . . .' and thus to encourage immigration only of 'young and courageous people, steeped in idealism, with a pioneering spirit and who are not afraid of hard physical work'.[57]

In spite of Zionist and British attempts to restrict immigration into Palestine by propaganda and reorganisation of the machinery of control, immigration into Palestine during the following months did not decline, but surprisingly increased even more.[58] This apparent paradox may be explained by examining the prevailing conditions in eastern Europe and the motives of Jews to immigrate to Palestine in particular.

Major Morris, Director of the Department of Immigration and Travel, who visited the immigration centres in Europe in summer 1921, met during his tour with local British Consuls, Zionist workers and personally examined hundreds of immigrants in an attempt to find out the reasons behind the British and Zionist failure to control immigration. In his report to Samuel, Morris mentions the following reasons for this situation: the United States of America had closed its gates to mass immigration which seriously affected Jewish immigration from eastern Europe. The American Joint Distribution Committee (Joint) suspended its relief work in these countries, which worsened the already difficult condition of the Jews there, particularly of the refugees from Russia and the Ukraine, who were concentrated in Poland and Rumania. Further on in the report, Morris describes the motives of the Zionist Offices to encourage immigration to Palestine by all means whether legal or otherwise, in order to keep their prestige and activities on a high level and 'to push on the development of the National Home by pouring in a continuous stream of immigrants'. Nevertheless, Morris ignored the responsibility for oversights in control of the British Consuls, who in his opinion were misled by the Zionists.

Leaving aside Morris's claims and accusations, it is still possible to conclude that the British and Zionist attempts to restrict immigration failed, because they did not conform with the original legal and administrative patterns which were set up with the intention of encouraging large scale immigration to Palestine. In order to bring about a radical change in the policy it was necessary to change these patterns and adapt them to a selective and more regulated system of control which was desirable to both the British and the Zionists.

Notes

[1] Samuel, *Memoirs,* p. 150.

[2] Ibid, p. 139.

[3] Stein, *The Balfour Declaration,* p. 138.

[4] Samuel, *Memoirs,* pp. 140-4; Weizmann, *Trial and Error* pp. 191-3.

[5] See Samuel's memorandum in Bowle, *Viscount Samuel — a Biography,* pp. 175-6.

[6] Stein, *The Balfour Declaration,* p. 139.

[7] Ibid, p. 116.

[8] Samuel, *Memoirs,* p. 148; on the various contacts previous to this visit, see letter of Richard Meinertzhagen, Political Officer at G.H.Q. Cairo to F.O. 2.12.19, I.S.A. 2/241; also Major General Bols, Military Administrator of Palestine to W.O., 21.12.19, F.O. 371/4426 file E164218/476/44.

[9] Aharon Aharonson, member of the Zionist Commission in Palestine had already noted in his diary in December 1918, that he was aware of a conversation between Weizmann and Lloyd George, in which the question of Samuel's appointment as High Commissioner of Palestine had arisen. Friesel, *Weizmann's First Steps,* p.118 also Medzini, *Esser Shanim,* p.134.

[10] Bowles, *Viscount Samuel,* pp. 189-90.

[11] Samuel, *Memoirs,* p. 150.

[12] Ibid, p. 151.

[13] See minutes of meeting, C.Z.A. Z4/3766. Zionist memorandum submitted to Samuel one day previous to the meeting was not found, but its main principles appear in the above-mentioned minutes.

[14] See Samuel's memorandum 'Immigration into Palestine', 16.6.20, F.O. 371/5183 file E6531/476/44.

[15] F.O. to Samuel (Jerusalem), 5.7.20, F.O. 371/5183, file E7141/764/44.

[16] Second in a long list of new Ordinances.

[17] See 'Military Regulations Governing Admission of Civilians into Palestine', 31.5.20, F.O. 371/5183, pp. 185-7. These Regulations were in actual fact of little significance as they were not enforced until one month before the setting up of the Civil Administration.

[18] Legal Secretary to Civil (Chief) Secretary, 29.7.20, I.S.A. 11/1.

[19] Ibid, ibid.

[20] F.O. to Samuel, 23.8.20, F.O. 371/5184 file E9773/476/44.

[21] See Appendix 1.

[22] See list of Major and Minor Departments of Palestine Government in I.S.A. 2/67 undated.

[23] See list of members of Advisory Council, C.O. 814/3.

[24] See note 13 above.

[25] £21,492 as against £2,286,133, the total estimated budget for the year 1921/22. Samuel to Curzon, 16.2.21, C.O. 733/1 file 10319.

[26] See 'Memorandum on Palestine Estimates 1921/22', C.O. 733/1 file 1204.

[27] See Chapter 5 below, pp. 86-7.

[28] Stein, *The Balfour Declaration, p. 104, p. 472.*

29 List of Immigration Department Officials, 5.12.20, C.O. 733/8 file 63945.

30 See Samuel to the Duke of Devonshire, Secretary of State for the Colonies, 1.6.23, C.O. 733/45 file 29427.

31 Nordau, *Zichronoth*, p. 274

32 Weizmann, *Trial and Error*, p. 327; Friesel, *Weizmann's First Steps*, pp. 123-44.

34 Minutes of Samuel's interview with members of Z.C., 2.7.20, I.S.A. 2/33.

35 Z.C. to Morris, 18.7.20, I.S.A. 11/3/3.

36 'Instructions to Consuls', 20.8.20, see Appendix 2.

37 See note 34 above.

38 See Appendix 5.

39 Dr. A. Sonne, who had been sent from London to Palestine to examine the Z.C.'s activities on the spot, in a report to Political Secretary, C.Z.O., 24.8.20, C.Z.A. Z4/1247.

40 Ibid, ibid.

41 Samuel to Curzon, 13.9.20, F.O. 406/44 file E11947/85/44.

42 Samuel to Curzon, 20.11.20, F.O. 371/5085 file E15029/476/44; also 17.12.20, F.O. 371/6382 file E440/144/88; ibid, E2346/144/88.

43 O.A. Scott of the Eastern Department, F.O. to Samuel Landman, General Secretary, C.Z.O., London, 3.8.20, C.Z.A. Z4/25004.

44 See F.O. instructions to H.M. Consuls in Europe, 15.7.20, F.O. 371/5184 file E7189/476/44.

45 Leonard Stein, Acting Political Secretary, C.Z.O., London in notes on interview with Parkin of Passport Department, F.O., 15.10.20, C.Z.A. Z4/963.

46 Samuel to F.O., tel. 195, 18.8.20, F.O.371/5184, file E10630/476/44.

47 O.A. Scott, F.O., minutes dated 25.8.20, ibid; also F.O. to Samuel 28.8.20, ibid.

48 R.T.Parkin, minutes dated 22.10.20, F.O. 371/5185 file E12987/476/44.

49 Parkin, minutes dated 26.10.20, ibid. Later on, he described these Zionist attempts to be 'a typical example of a Dead Sea red herring', minutes, 9.12.20, F.O. 371/5185, file E1503/476/44.

50 L. Stein to F.O. 18.10.20, F.O. 371/5185 file E12987/476/44.

51 Parkin's notes on meeting with Stein, 22.10.20, ibid.

52 C.Z.O. to F.O., F.O. 371/5185 file E15909/476/44.

53 See Appendix 5.

54 See relevant correspondence in F.O. 371/6382 files E1469 E1573/144/88.

55 'Instructions concerning immigration into Palestine', Circular No. 1, London, 15.10.20, Z4/1287.

56 C.Z.O., circular to Palestine Offices, 19.11.20, ibid.

57 C.Z.O., circular to Palestine Offices, 17.12.20, ibid.

58 4,995 immigrants during the first five months of the Civil Administration in comparison with 5,657 immigrants during the five following months, see Appendix 5.

Chapter Two

THE TURNING POINT — TEMPORARY SUSPENSION OF IMMIGRATION

THE PALESTINE PHASE

The failure of the Zionist Organisation during the first year of Civil Administration to raise sufficient funds for the economic absorption of immigrants, most of whom were without independent means, finally brought about a radical change in immigration policy. The outlining of the revised policy lasted for the duration of Samuel's rule in Palestine and was a result of political, administrative, legal and economic considerations which will be dealt with respectively in the following chapters. However, the turning point of the immigration policy — the temporary suspension of Jewish immigration — was a direct consequence of the political crisis in Palestine following the May Disturbances. This distinction requires that the two episodes be dealt with separately.

The Disturbances, which broke out in Jaffa on May Day 1921 and spread over the neighbouring areas during the following week, forced Samuel into a confrontation with violent Arab opposition which he had feared and tried to prevent during his first ten months in office.[1] In spite of a gradual increase in political tension, which followed the third Arab Palestinian Congress in December 1920, the Administration was neither mentally nor physically prepared for the extent and intensity of the outbreaks. In addition to a

17

demand to set up representative self-government in Palestine as in Iraq and Trans-Jordan, the Arab Congress passed anti-Zionist resolutions calling for the immediate abolition of: the Balfour Declaration policy; the recognition of the Zionist Organisation as an official body; the use of Hebrew as an official language; the services of known Zionists in senior posts in the Administration and suspension of all Jewish immigration. The Congress elected an Executive whose duty was to see to the fulfilment of these demands.[2]

The short visit of the Colonial Secretary, Winston Churchill, to Palestine in March 1921, gave the Arab Executive an exceptional opportunity to promote its political aims. But, for the Arabs, the meeting with Churchill was disappointing, if not downright insulting. In the first place, he refused to see a delegation of the Executive which had come to Cairo and would only agree to see them in Jerusalem. When he finally received them, he told them frankly that the present form of Government would continue for many years, declaring that 'our children's children will have passed away by the time that [full self-government] is completed'. Concerning the Arab demand to abolish the Balfour Declaration and to veto Jewish immigration, Churchill's reply was short and blunt: 'It is not in my power to do so, nor if it were in my power would it be my wish.'[3] Churchill's reaction to the demands of the Arab delegation probably did little towards easing the political tension in the country.[4] It is very likely that Arab extremists began to seek another more convincing means of showing their objection to the Government's Zionist policy.[5]

After the festival of Nebi Musa in April, an event prone to trouble, had passed by peacefully, the May Day outbreak was totally unexpected.[6] During the first few days of the Disturbances Samuel remained composed, apparently in the belief that the outburst was incidental and confined to the Jaffa area.[7] This might explain his refusal to declare martial law in Jaffa from the outset, contrary to the opinion of his senior advisers who were on the spot.[8] When finally forced by the Army to declare martial law,[9] he limited this to the Jaffa district only, and thus the violence later spread to other districts. At this stage, Samuel was endeavouring to avoid direct and violent clashes with the rioters, preferring more demonstrative action such as the presence of warships of the Mediterranean Fleet facing the coast of Palestine, and constant patrolling by aircraft as a demonstration of strength, in order to prevent a renewal of the outbreaks.[10]

The question of immigration was at the centre of events right from the very beginning of the outbreaks. The two demonstrations, one of a Jewish Socialist party and the other of the Communists, which clashed on May Day and indirectly caused the outbreak of the incidents, were composed of young Jewish pioneers, mostly new immigrants.[11] The first Arab attack, which claimed the largest number of Jewish victims, was directed not unintentionally at the Immigrants House in Jaffa, 'as an emblem of Jewish immigration'.[12] Arab boatmen at the port of Jaffa, who took an active part in the disturbances, made clear their opposition to further disembarkation of immigrants;[13] Arab leaders, while officially disapproving of the attacks and expressing 'sorrow', 'regret' and 'sympathy' to the relatives of victims,[14] utilized them for their own political purposes. Musa Kazim el Husaini, President of the Arab Executive, sent letters to a long list of personages and institutions in Great Britain and Europe, describing the spread of Bolshevism propagated by Jewish immigrants, as an inevitable consequence of the Balfour Declaration policy.[15]

The focusing of Arab agitation on the question of Jewish immigration and Jewish Communists led Samuel to deal first and foremost with these two topics. Action against the Communists, a small outcast group, with no roots in Palestine and entirely lacking in public support, was speedy and efficient. On the first day of the incidents, Samuel issued appropriate instructions to prepare for the arrest and deportation of the Communist ringleaders, which began on 9 March, as well as searches for the Communists who had gone underground in the meantime.[16]

Settling the immigration question was a far more delicate and complicated matter. Despite heavy Arab pressure in favour of suspending immigration immediately, Samuel would not give in. On the fourth day of the rioting, he still assured the Zionists that immigration would not be stopped.[17] On the same day, when a slight lull gave the impression that the incidents were at an end, 150 Jewish immigrants were brought ashore at Jaffa under the protection of the Army and taken to Tel-Aviv.[18] In addition, a further 30-odd immigrants were allowed to enter Palestine clandestinely via Egypt.[19] These facts contradict the generally accepted version that immigration was automatically suspended with the outbreak of the incidents.

Furthermore, during the first five days, Samuel attempted to find various alternative means of entry for the immigrants, without antagonising the Arabs and giving them a further pretext for continuing the disturbances.[20] One possibility was to let the immigrants off at Haifa, the other available port in Palestine. Although the situation in Haifa was still quiet, the Haifa District Governor stated that he could not take responsibility for public order if Jewish immigrants were to land there.[21]

Another alternative was to disembark the immigrants in Egypt and wait for the storm to subside before bringing them into Palestine. On 4 May, Samuel applied urgently to Allenby, the British High Commissioner in Egypt, asking for temporary accommodation at Port Said or Alexandria for about 300 Jewish immigrants expected that week.[22] Allenby refused, explaining that the political situation in Egypt at that time did not allow this and suggested sending them back to their port of embarkation.[23] Samuel did not despair and reapplied to Allenby on the following day, this time asking only that the parties be allowed to land at Port Said and sent on immediately by train via Kantara to Palestine.[24] This possibility also came to nothing.

In the meantime, from the fifth day of the outbreaks, the situation in the country was becoming worse. 'The facts of the Jaffa riots', stated the official report of the Committee of Inquiry into the disturbances, 'were greatly exaggerated and there were stories of Moslem men, women and children having been murdered by the Jews'. These rumours put the Arabs in a high state of excitement.[25] In districts north and south of Jaffa, Arab raids were launched on Jewish colonies and without the immediate and effective intervention of the Army, the whole country might have been dragged into a civil war.[26] It would seem that these developments, accompanied by grim reports from the District Governors,[27] changed Samuel's opinion of the character and extent of the disturbances. He then came to the conclusion that the Arab movement was 'a deep national movement', and the outbreaks 'a war of the Arab nation against the Hebrew nation' and not 'just the propaganda of a small band', as the Zionists endeavoured to describe them.[28]

It was presumably at this stage that Samuel decided to suspend immigration, including the clandestine infiltration of immigrants under Government auspices. The S.S. 'Sicilia', which arrived at Jaffa on 5 May with 26 Jewish immigrants on board, and the S.S. 'Georgovia' on 7 May, received permission to disembark all their passengers, with the exception of Jewish immigrants. The S.S. 'Dalmatia' with 165 immigrants on board, which arrived the following day, was instructed to proceed to Port Said.[29]

However, the unofficial stoppage of immigration did not completely satisfy the Arabs, who pressed for an official proclamation on the suspension of immigration.[30] On 6 May, huge crowds of Arabs had gathered in Ramle at a festival for Nebi Salih, threatening to attack Jewish settlements in the neighbourhood.[31] The High Commissioner instructed the District Governor by telephone to announce there, that there would be no more immigration for the time being.[32] Although this declaration came from a figure of secondary importance, and there was no assurance that it had actually come from the High Commissioner, it caused a general furore among the Jews in Palestine.[33] Rumours spread that the intention had been not only to suspend immigration, but not to renew it and to return all Jewish immigrants thus far in Palestine to their countries of origin.[34] At any rate, if it was Samuel's intention to try out the effect of this statement on the Arabs, he was to see an opposite effect than the one hoped for. Part of the Arab crowd, encouraged by the Government's concessions to their demands, attacked Jewish settlements in the area.[35]

Samuel's decision to make a public announcement on suspension of immigration brought to a head the tension between himself and the Zionists. In frequent meetings with

Samuel and other senior officials, Zionist representatives used diverse and sometimes conflicting arguments in a supreme effort to prevent an official change in immigration policy. From the humanitarian point of view they emphasised the suffering of the immigrants, among them women and children who, having reached the shores of Palestine after months in transit, were to be subjected to further hardships.[36] Morally, they considered this suspension to be a crude denial of British promises and a hard blow to the principles of the mandate, likely to bring about a loss of confidence in the British on the part of the Jewish people all over the world.[37]

From a political point of view, the Jewish leaders maintained that 'there is no question about freedom of immigration. It is a basic [Jewish] right, which even the Turks had not been able to infringe'. 'Change of immigration policy', as far as they were concerned, 'will be the downfall of Zionism' or a 'mortal blow to the Zionists, which would cause despair throughout the Yishuv'.[38]

Of all their arguments, perhaps the most interesting were those which attempted to guide Samuel through the mysteries of oriental politics and help him to extricate himself from the complications arising out of his 'weak policy'. Yet the Zionists themselves had difficulty in grasping the situation clearly and unequivocally. On one occasion, they claimed that the outbursts were 'the propaganda of a small band';[39] on another, they were at pains to convince Samuel that the riots had not been spontaneous but planned in advance by Arab leaders.[40] The Zionists, having always maintained that the Arabs did not hate the Jews, were now undecided as to how they should interpret the riots: were they to be seen as proof of deep-seated animosity?[41]

Despite the Zionists' difficulty in arriving at an accurate analysis of the events, throughout all their contacts with the Government they were consistent in their demands for firmer action on the part of the Administration and the Army and for more severe punishment of the rioters, explaining that this would be the only means of a speedy end to the rioting. According to the Zionists, concessions on immigration policy would not pacify the Arabs but would, on the contrary, be interpreted as 'a justification for their deeds and a proof of weakness of the Government . . . and will increase their appetite for more'.[42] The conclusion towards which they were attempting to direct the British, was that 'the victory of the Arabs will arouse in them the desire for still more and they will soon arise not only against the Jews, but also against the British rule, which they desire to rid themselves of'.[43]

As a reaction to Samuel's intentions to appease the Arabs on immigration policy, a consistent change in the tone and vigour of the Zionist demands became apparent. At first, they encouraged Samuel not to give in to Arab pressure to suspend immigration.[44] Once aware of his difficulties, they suggested disembarking the immigrants in Egypt and bringing them into Palestine secretly and even offered to help organise this operation.[45] However, when it became apparent that this was not realistic because of Allenby's refusal to let the immigrants land in Egypt, they insisted that they be allowed to land openly at Jaffa, with the protection of the Army 'to prove the authority of the Government'.[46]

When it became obvious that Samuel was about to declare an official suspension of immigration, a proposal was made at one of the Zionist meetings in favour of anticipating Samuel and declaring that the Jews had decided to stop immigration 'in view of the abnormal situation'.[47] This suggestion was finally rejected, apparently so that the Arabs should not interpret it as a sign of weakness on the Jewish side.

The high state of frustration and despair which had overcome the Jewish leadership in Palestine during those emotional days, may be well illustrated by the two following examples. On the eighth day of the outbreaks, after an additional interview with Samuel had ended in failure, Nahum Sokolow, the moderate Chairman of the Zionist Executive, suggested opening a 'large criminal case which would become a national spectacle, on the lines of the Damascus blood-libel trial or the Bayliss trial . . .'[48]

The following day, Dr. Eder, the Political Secretary of the Zionist Commission, wrote to Joseph Cowen, member of the

Zionist Executive in London: 'If the High Commissioner's reply re: immigration is negative, it is the intention of the Zionist Commission and Jewish bodies to resign. I have another policy in my mind, to ask the British Government to resign, to give up the mandate in Palestine, since they cannot carry out minimum thereof. Not to ask any country to mandate but to leave us Jews to have it out ourselves with the Arabs. I reckon we have 10,000 men capable of bearing arms in the country . . . If we have to lose Palestine, I would rather we went down fighting than were gradually extinguished. However, perhaps all this is unnecessary, we may get a firm answer from Herbert Samuel'.[49]

The Zionists did not receive a 'firm answer' from Samuel. A threat to bring about a collective resignation of the leading Jewish bodies in Palestine — the Jewish National Council, the Zionist Commission and the Rabbinate — was counteracted by Samuel's own threat to resign.[50]

Meanwhile, Samuel concluded his deliberations and began outlining a new policy aimed at pacifying the Arabs and channelling their political initiative towards constructive lines within a new constitutional framework.[51] In the meantime, to prevent a renewal of the outbreaks he applied urgently to the Colonial Office for permission to announce that he would make a statement at the King's Birthday Assembly on 3 June, upon 'certain important constitutional and administrative measures which the Government is about to adopt with a view to establishing harmony amongst the people', in the hope that this announcement 'will induce all sections to adopt a waiting attitude'.[52] However, before approval from London had arrived, he was informed by the Military Governor in Jaffa that the situation was changing for the worse and at any moment disturbances might break out again.[53] Samuel did not delay, but cancelled the original announcement and hastened that same night to instruct all District Governors to publicize a fresh announcement confirming the suspension of immigration, which had actually been in effect for ten days.[54]

THE LONDON PHASE

The first news of the riots in Jaffa did not reach the Colonial

Office until the following day, and then by means of a telephone call from a news agency.[55] An official version from Jerusalem did not arrive until the day after. Samuel's report, although giving the large number of victims of the first two days (40 dead and 170 wounded), pointed out that 'it was not found necessary to proclaim martial law',[56] which gave the impression that he was in full command of the situation.[57] Churchill's reaction was that Samuel should take strong action and 'bring to justice persons guilty of murderous violence'.[58]

The correspondence between Samuel and Lord Allenby during the first week of the disturbances concerning the disembarkation of Jewish immigrants in Egypt, was brought to the attention of the Colonial and the Foreign Offices. The Foreign Office decided not to take action as long as the Colonial Office did not request it.[59] It seems that lack of support on the part of the Colonial Office for Samuel's demands, left intact Allenby's refusal to allow immigrants to land in Egypt.

During that critical week, when the Jewish leadership in Palestine was struggling against suspension of immigration, there had been no parallel initiative on the part of the Zionist Executive in London. It was only after the first round of contacts in Jerusalem had ended dismally for the Zionists, that the Zionist Executive was stirred into action. Yet, unaware of Samuel's intention to suspend immigration, they were unable to act accordingly. Instead, following reports in the British press which gave the impression that 'the whole matter was the work of the Jewish Bolsheviks',[60] the Zionist Executive devoted its efforts towards warding off these attacks. To this end, Samuel Landman and Joseph Cowen, members of the Zionist Executive, met Churchill in an attempt to dispel any rumours of connection between the Communist demonstration and the subsequent riots. The Zionists asked Churchill to explain these facts in a public statement, emphasising that 'the number of Jewish communists in Palestine was insignificant'. Churchill agreed and promised to 'bear in mind' the matter of the statement.[61]

It was at this meeting that the Zionist Executive first learned of Samuel's intention to suspend immigration. However, it seems that the Executive was misled by the Colonial Office, who gave them to understand that the Zionist Commission had agreed to the suspension of immigration.[62] Accordingly, the Zionist Executive cabled to Jerusalem, expressing their strong opposition to the suspension, stating that 'if the Government wishes to stop immigration, they must do it upon their own responsibility and that it should be quite understood by them that they are doing it against our wishes'.[63]

This situation raises some important questions: how could the Zionist Executive in London not have known about the suspension of immigration a whole week after it had been enforced, nor of Samuel's intention to approve this policy officially in the form of a declaration? Why did the Zionist Commission not demand the immediate intervention of the Zionist Executive at the Colonial Office to avoid such a declaration?

First, one should remember that until 5 May, despite strong Arab opposition, immigration was not suspended and Jewish leaders were assured by Samuel that he had no intention of doing so. After immigration had nevertheless been suspended unofficially, they still hoped that Samuel would refrain from making an official declaration.[64] Second, the Jewish leaders in Palestine wished to emphasise the national character of their campaign against the suspension of immigration. The Jewish National Council (Hava'ad Haleumi), which played a major role here, was a sovereign body of the Yishuv and was not reliant in any way upon the Zionist Executive in London. Third, Nahum Sokolow, Chairman of the Zionist Executive and second most important personality after Weizmann in the leadership of the Movement, was in Palestine at that time and conducted all negotiations with the Administration personally. Weizmann, whose presence either in London or in Palestine was vital, was then in the United States of America. There were no other prominent Zionist leaders in London at that time.

Once Jewish leaders in Palestine realised that they would be unable to change Samuel's decision on their own, they cabled to London, reporting in detail on their negotiations with the Administration and asked for the support of the Executive in order to renew immigration and avoid official suspension. This telegram, despatched on 10 May, did not reach London until three days later, which gives the impression that it was held back by the Administration.[65] The report from Jerusalem stimulated the Zionist Executive to reopen intensive contacts both with the Colonial Office and with the Foreign Office for a dual purpose: to issue a pro-Zionist statement and to prevent repatriation of immigrants who had been refused entry to Palestine.

Once Churchill had agreed in principle to make the statement, the Zionists were asked to prepare a draft and present it to the Colonial Office for approval and publication. The Zionist Executive requested that the suspension of immigration into Palestine should be defined as a 'purely temporary measure' and that 'the establishment of a Jewish National Home in that country has not been and will not be shaken by the resort to violence of certain elements among the population of Palestine'.[66] The statement was intended both for external and internal needs. Externally, to incline public opinion in Britain more towards the Zionists and to counteract the 'distorted' information which had appeared in the press; internally, to calm the uproar among the Zionist world and restore confidence in its leadership.[67]

The second objective, to prevent repatriation of immigrants to Europe, was far more complicated. Following the official suspension of immigration, Samuel still continued in his attempts to obtain Allenby's permission to accommodate immigrants in Egypt temporarily.[68] However, the intensification of hostility towards the British in Egypt and the local demonstrations against landing Jewish immigrants there, apparently made it inexpedient for Allenby to accede to Samuel's request.[69]

Simultaneously with Samuel's efforts, the Zionists in London were exerting pressure on the Colonial Office and the Foreign Office in a last minute attempt to revoke Allenby's decision to return the 158 Jewish immigrants aboard the S.S. 'Dalmatia' to Constantinople. Officials of the Colonial Office who were not convinced of the 'weight of Allenby's reasons' for not keeping these immigrants in

Egypt, supported the Zionist demand and also applied to the Foreign Office. At the same time, they did not entirely discard the possibility of exerting pressure on Samuel to allow these immigrants, already en route, to land in Palestine or at least to arrange for them to enter by train via Kantara.[70] However, all the efforts of the Zionist Executive proved fruitless. Colonial Office officials failed to persuade their colleagues at the Foreign Office to intervene and change Allenby's decision.

Once the Zionists realised that their attempts to gain permission for the immigrants to land in Egypt had failed, they focused their efforts on obtaining the protection of British Consuls for immigrants who were to be returned to their ports of exit.[71] Here the Zionists achieved more positive results. The Foreign Office sent instructions to its representatives in Europe to give their 'best assistance' to the local Zionist Offices concerning these immigrants, but to avoid providing any financial help.[72] However, these instructions could not prevent the increasing chaos amongst thousands of immigrants already en route. The blame must, at least in part, be attributed to the British Administration for not sending appropriate instructions in time. A whole week had passed between the suspension of immigration and Samuel's application to the Colonial Office requesting the Foreign Office to instruct Consuls to stop granting visas. This telegram was delayed at the Colonial Office for five days before being passed on to the Foreign Office, which did not send out the necessary instructions until four days later.[73]

During this time, over 3,000 immigrants had arrived at ports and main cities in Eastern Europe, most of them furnished with British visas for Palestine.[74] Because of this situation, Samuel urgently sent two Immigration Officers to Europe to control and regulate immigration on the spot.

MORRIS'S MISSION — THE CONTINENT PHASE

On 9 June, Major Morris, Director of the Palestine Immigration Department, and his assistant, Nathan Mindel, left for Europe. They had been instructed to investigate each immigrant and check carefully the reliability of his papers and his suitability for immigration from an economic and political point of view. They were to pay particular attention to preventing the infiltration of Bolsheviks or any other extremist elements, with full authority to refuse those who did not satisfy them.[75]

However, the main objective of this mission was to regulate immigration so that immigrants would arrive in Palestine in small groups of no more than 100 people and would come in through three points of entry: Jaffa, Haifa and Kantara, at reasonable intervals of time. For this purpose the Immigration Officers had to classify the immigrants according to their date of arrival, ports of exit, the extent of their mobility and economic viability. First priority was given to single men, then to families and lastly to women and children on their own. This method was not so much humanitarian as practical, so as to facilitate their disembarkation and speedy dispersal in Palestine. To this end, the Administration enlisted the help of the Zionist Commission to organise the secret and speedy transfer of immigrants, in groups of 50 persons, directly to Jewish colonies.[76]

At Constantinople and Trieste, the situation was at its worst, as the immigrants had been there the longest and those who had been refused permission to disembark in Palestine and Egypt had been returned to these two ports. For this reason the Immigration Officers were sent there first: Mindel to Trieste and Morris to Constantinople. Samuel instructed them to request the assistance of the local Zionist Organisation and British Consuls upon their arrival and asked the Foreign Office for the co-operation of its representative wherever the Officers intended to visit.[77]

At Constantinople, Morris found about 500 immigrants. In accordance with given instructions, he interviewed only those holding British visas and rejected the rest — about 350 persons — on the spot. Of those holding British visas, he refused about half, who had obtained visas on the grounds that they were 'self-supporting', but who had not really fulfilled the required conditions of having either enough money or definite employment.[78] The rest, most of them immigrants who had obtained guarantees from the Zionist Organisation before obtaining their British visa, were issued with fresh visas and divided into two groups which were given permission to leave for Palestine at an interval of two weeks.[79]

At Constantinople, Morris was able to follow at first hand the activities of the Zionist Offices in Eastern Europe. In his view, these were influenced by the dual and sometimes conflicting functions of the Organisation: on the one hand to promote immigration to Palestine and on the other to select the immigrants. At this time of crisis, such a contradiction stood out more than ever, since, following the suspension, the Zionists felt their prestige shaken with the likely consequence that immigration and subscriptions for Palestine would drop significantly.[80]

At Vienna, the number of immigrants was much higher and pressure exerted on Morris thus stronger. Here, the Zionists did not concern themselves only with problems of prestige and distrust, but with more concrete difficulties such as the financial burden of housing and maintaining about 900 immigrants and a worsening of relations with the Austrian authorities.[81] Austria, the main transit country for emigration from eastern Europe, threatened to close its gates to further Jewish immigration unless the Zionists could carry out their undertaking that immigrants would remain no longer than three weeks. This threat materialised after Morris had rejected a third of the immigrants he had examined and Poland had objected to their repatriation.[82]

From Vienna, Morris continued to Budapest and Warsaw and from there via Berlin to Trieste. Out of 3,400 immigrants en route, 1,550 immigrants in possession of British visas were interviewed by him and Mindel. About two thirds — 1,058 — were permitted to proceed to Palestine and 542 were refused.[83] Morris's hope that a delay would cause most of the 2,000 rejected immigrants to return to their own countries, did not materialise.[84] The refusal of the Governments of Poland and Rumania to repatriate the immigrants left them no other choice but to wait at the ports of exit, until the normalization of immigration policy in September allowed them to proceed to Palestine.

The attitude of prospective Polish immigrants was completely different. Out of 2,000 in possession of British

visas only 300 came to be interviewed, which confirmed
Morris's assumption that the disturbances in Palestine and
suspension of immigration had an entirely different effect on
Jews still in their homes, than on those already en route.[85]
This brought Morris to his main conclusions: first, that only
efficient machinery of control on the spot would select and
regulate immigration in accordance with the economic conditions in Palestine and second, that this control should be
transferred from the Zionist Organisation to officers directly
subordinate to the Immigration Department in Jerusalem.[86]

NOTES

[1] Caplan, *The Yishuv,* pp. 133-8.

[2] Porath, *The Emergence,* pp. 108-10.

[3] See Churchill's reply to the Arab Delegation, 28.3.21, C.O.733/2 file
21689.

[4] See report of Captain C.D. Brunton of General Staff Intelligence on
effects of Churchill's visit on Arab spirits in Palestine. 'Churchill', wrote
Brunton, 'upheld the Zionist cause and treated the Arab demands like
those of a negligible opposition to be put off by a few political phrases and
treated like bad children'. 13.5.21, C.O.733/13 file 32993. Churchill,
typically, was quite unafraid to present this report to the Cabinet; 9.6.21,
ibid.

[5] Porath, *The Emergence,* pp. 128-9.

[6] 'Report on Political Situation in Palestine, April 1921', 9.5.21,
C.O.733/3 file 24596; see also Dr. David Eder of the Zionist Commission,
Jerusalem, to the Zionist Executive in London, 28.4.21, in Friesel,
Weizmann, p. 260.

[7] Ruppin, following an interview with the H.C. on second day of
outbreak, Ruppin, *Memoirs,* p. 191.

[8] Wyndham Deedes, the Chief Secretary, who went immediately to Jaffa
and Colonel Sterling, the Jaffa District Governor. See Samuel's long and
detailed report to Churchill on the May Disturbances, 15.5.21, (Samuel's
Report) despatch 107, C.O.733/3 file 25835.

[9] Ibid, ibid.

[10] Ibid, ibid.

[11] Dinur, *Hahagana,* Vol.B, Part I, p. 79.

[12] Abcarius, *Palestine,* P.75; Dinur, *Hahagana,* pp. 80-1.

[13] Ibid, p. 112.

[14] See minutes of the 8th meeting of the Advisory Council, 3.5.21,
C.O.733/3 file 24594.

[15] Musa Kazim el Husaini to the Speaker of the House of Commons with
copies to H.M. King George V, His Holiness the Pope, the Speaker of the

House of Lords, and the Foreign Secretaries of Great Britain, France Italy, Spain and the United States of America, 3.5.21, C.O.733/16 file 23918; also Omar Betar, President of the Moslem Christian Committee, Jaffa, to H.M. King George V, 12.5.21, C.O.733/16 file 24124.

[16] Samuel's Report 15.5.21, C.O.733/3 file 25835.

[17] Eder's interview with Samuel, 4.5.21, C.Z.A. J1/138.

[18] Dinur, *Hahagana,* p. 83.

[19] 'Administration Report, June 1921', 4.7.21, C.O.733/4 file 34950.

[20] Samuel's Report, 15.5.21, P.R.O., C.O.733/3 file 25835.

[21] V.L.E. interview with Civil Secretary, 7.5.21, C.Z.A. J1/138.

[22] Lord Allenby to F.O., 4.5.21, Tel. 279 'very urgent'. F.O. 371/6382 file E5248/144/88

[23] Allenby, addressed to Jerusalem, repeated to F.O., 4.5.21, F.O. 371/6382 file E5249/144/88.

[24] H.C. for Palestine to Allenby, Cairo 5.5.21, I.S.A. 11/3/3.

[25] Cmd. 1540, p. 5.

[26] Ibid., ibid.

[27] Samuel's report, 15.5.21, C.O.733/3 file 25835.

[28] See Sokolow's report to a joint session of the V.L.E., and Z.C., regarding his interview with the H.C., 8.5.21, C.Z.A., J1/139.

[29] Memo of Imm. Dept., 8.5.21., I.S.A. 11/3; also 'Situation in Palestine' enclosed in Samuel's despatch to C.O., 8.5.21, C.O.733/3 file 24660.

[30] Minutes of meeting with the H.C., 5.5.21, C.Z.A. J1/138.

[31] Medzini, *Esser Shanim,* p. 180.

[32] Dr. D. Eder in V.L.E. meeting with Sokolow, 8.5.21, C.Z.A. J1/139.

[33] Medzini, *Esser Shanim,* p. 180.

[34] Minutes of V.L.E. meeting with Sokolow, 8.5.21, C.Z.A. J1/139; see also V.L.E. petition to the H.C., 10.5.21, in Attias, *Sefer ha-Teudot*, pp. 56-7.

[35] Dinur, *Hahagana,* pp. 90-1.

[36] Attias, *Sefer ha-Teudot,* pp. 56-7.

[37] Y. Ben-Zvi, member of V.L.E., in his letter to the H.C. regarding his resignation from the Palestine Advisory Council, 11.5.21, Attias, p. 60.

[38] Y. Thon, member of V.L.E. in an interview with the Chief Secretary, 7.5.21, C.Z.A. J1/139; Sokolow in joint session of V.L.E. and Z.C., 8.5.21, ibid; Y. Ben-Zvi in his letter of resignation, see note 37 above.

[39] See note 28 above.

[40] Y. Ben-Zvi in V.L.E. interview with the H.C., 5.5.21, C.Z.A. J1/139.

[41] See minutes of V.L.E. and Z.C., joint session, 9.5.21, ibid.

[42] Y. Thon, see note 40 above.

[43] Ibid, ibid.

[44] Dr. D. Eder in interview with the H.C., 4.5.21, C.Z.A. J1/138.

[45] Minutes of V.L.E. meeting with the H.C., see note 40 above.

[46] D. Yellin, member of V.L.E. in joint meeting with Z.C., see note 38 above.

[47] Minutes of V.L.E. — Z.C. meeting, 9.5.21, C.Z.A. J1/139.

[48] V.L.E. meeting with Sokolow, 8.5.21, ibid.

[49] Dr. Eder to J. Cowen, private, 9.5.21., C.Z.A. Z4/16151.

[50] See note 47 above.

[51] Samuel to Churchill, 8.5.21, despatch 82, confidential C.O.733/3 file 24660.

[52] Samuel to Churchill, 12.5.21, tel. 151, F.O.371/6382, file E5685/144/88.

[53] Samuel to Churchill, 13.5.21, tel. 155, C.O.733/3, file 23789.

[54] H.C. to Jaffa District Governor, 13.5.21, On the following day all other Governors were given instructions I.S.A. 2/144.

[55] See minutes, Middle East Dept., C.O., 2.5.21., C.O.733/3, file 21723.

[56] Samuel to Churchill, 2.5.21, ibid.

[57] See minutes of Middle East Dept., C.O., 3.5.21, ibid.

[58] Churchill to Samuel, 3.5.21, ibid.

[59] J. Murry of Eastern Department, F.O., minutes, 4.5.21, F.O.371/6382 file E5249/144/88.

[60] See minutes of Z.E. meeting, 4.5.21, C.Z.A. Z4/302/4A.

[61] See minutes of interview with Churchill, 9.5.21, ibid.

[62] It seems that Churchill did not draw a very distinct picture to the Zionists of Samuel's steps regarding Jewish immigration. See Z.E. letter asking for more information on suspension of immigration, S. Landman to Secretary of State, C.O., 10.5.21, C.Z.A. L3/31.

[63] J. Cowen, Z.E. London, to Dr. Eder, Z.C. Jerusalem, 11.5.21, C.Z.A. S6/269.

[64] See Sokolow's report on interviews with Samuel and Deedes, V.L.E. meeting with Z.C., 8.5.21, C.Z.A. J1/139.

[65] See telegram signed by Sokolow, Ruppin, Eder, to Z.E. London, despatched 10.5.21, received 13.5.21, C.Z.A. Z4/302/4A.

[66] See draft Statement, 17.5.21, C.O. 733/16 file 24338.

[67] See copy cable sent to [Zionist] Federations, 14.5.21, C.Z.A., L3/31.

[68] Allenby to F.O. — 'received yesterday [13.5.21] from Jerusalem, Tel. 327' — 14.5.21, F.O. 371/6382 file E5590/144/88.

[69] Allenby to Samuel repeated to F.O. 14.5.21, F.O. 371/6382 file E5591/144/88. Samuel received confirmation on Allenby's difficulties from his own man, see C. Lambert, Palestine Immigration Officer in Kantara to Director of Immigration Department on riots in Alexandria, to which he was witness, 24.5.21, I.S.A. 11/3. Nevertheless, contrary to general belief (see *Hahagana*, p. 112), it seems that Allenby allowed a limited number of immigrants to land in Egypt until 10th May, see Palestine Administration Report for July, 8.8.21, C.O.733/5 file 42315.

[70] S. Landman to Major Young of C.O., 16.5.21, Young's minutes, 18.5.21, C.O.733/16 file 24067; S. Landman to Forbes-Adam of F.O. 16.5.21, F.O.371/6382 file E5670/144/88. J. Murry of F.O., minutes 17.5.21, F.O.371/6382 file E5608/144/88.

[71] J. Murry's minutes, 19.5.21, F.O.371/6382 file E5608/144/88.

[72] See the instructions, 21.5.21, ibid.

[73] H.C. for Palestine to Secretary of State for Colonies, 11.5.21, tel. 148; G. Grindel of C.O. to F.O., 17.5.21; F.O. to H.M.'s Representatives 21.5.21, all in F.O.371/6382 file E5685/144/88.

[74] See memo of Immigration Department, 14.6.21, I.S.A. 11/3/3.

[75] See 'Instructions regarding immigrants awaiting admission to Palestine', 8.6.21, ibid.

[76] ibid, ibid.

[77] H.C. for Palestine to C.O., tel. 212, 8.6.21, I.S.A., 11/3/3, also in C.Z.A., S6/269.

[78] Morris to H.C. for Palestine [21.7.21], I.S.A. 11/3/3; Morris's final and official report (Morris's Report), p.2, 18.8.21, C.O.733/6 file 47584.

[79] Morris to Passport Control Officer in Constantinople, 23.6.21, I.S.A. 11/3/3.

[80] Morris to H.C. for Palestine, [21.7.21], I.S.A., 11/3/3.

[81] Robert Stricker and Dr. Martin Rosenbluth of the Zionist Office in Vienna to Major Morris 26.6.21, I.S.A. 11/3/3.

[82] S.L. Schmid from the Austrian F.O., to Mr. Keeling of the British Embassy in Vienna, 5.7.21, I.S.A. 11/3.

[83] See memo of the Palestine Immigration Department, 27.8.21, I.S.A. 11/3/3.

[84] See note 78 above.

[85] Ibid, ibid.

[86] See the Conclusions of Morris's Report, pp. 22-3, 18.8.21, C.O.733/6 file 47584.

Chapter Three

REVIEW OF IMMIGRATION POLICY: THE ROAD TO THE WHITE PAPER

OUTLINING OF NEW SCHEMES OF CONTROL

During the first week of May a new immigration policy was beginning to take shape in Jerusalem.[1] The lesson of the Disturbances obliged Samuel to take a great deal more notice in the future of two principles which, in his view, had not been considered strictly enough until then: 'First, that the enterprises in which the men are to be engaged should be ready before the arrival of the immigrants; and second, that stricter control is kept over the selection of immigrants, individually, with a view to ensure the exclusion of those who are politically undesirable.'[2] In fact, these two methods were intended to achieve the same goal, namely to prevent the creation of a discontented nucleus, which was having difficulty in establishing itself in Palestine and liable to form a troublesome element.

In accordance with Samuel's instructions, the Department of Immigration and Travel under the supervision of Major Morris began working on a new scheme of control. By the end of May the first draft was ready. According to the new scheme, the Palestine Administration was to be assigned almost full and exclusive control over immigration at its sources. For this purpose, it was suggested that several Palestine Immigration Officers be appointed at the principal immigration centres in Europe. These Officers would carry

35

out all the functions previously exercised by the British consuls and the local branches of the Zionist Organisation regarding immigration.[3]

The advantages of the new system, as indicated by Morris himself, were as follows: first, it would enable all examinations and investigations concerning the applicant to be made near his domicile, which would give better insight into his political background, the reliability of his papers and the state of his health before he left for Palestine. Second, Palestine Immigration Officers well acquainted with the conditions there, would be in a better position than British consuls to fit the potential immigrants into the country's economic requirements. And third, 'the inhabitants of Palestine will be satisfied that immigration is properly controlled and that numbers are only allowed to come in as the development of the country demands.'[4]

The main political significance of the new method was the obvious ousting of the Zionist Organisation from its dominant position in the control of labour immigration. Its role in the new scheme was rather indistinct, and generally defined as to 'co-operate with the Administration in the selection of immigrants'. However, anticipating strong Zionist objection to the proposed scheme, Morris suggested that the Immigration Officers 'should be in sympathy with the Zionist cause' and that it should be made clear to the Zionist Organisation that they would benefit by having many expenses saved to them and the immigrants.[5]

The Zionist Commission was not associated with, nor informed of, the new scheme. In spite of its frequent meetings with Samuel during May, it was unable to extract any information on the future policy except a general promise that immigration would soon be resumed, but with 'stricter control according to the Economic Absorptive Capacity of Palestine'.[6] Samuel's forthright criticism of the Zionists' failure to absorb immigration did little towards easing their anxiety. Nevertheless, a general tranquillity in the country towards the end of May, and an improvement in the atmosphere between them and Samuel, aroused in them hopes that the new policy, to be made public on 3rd June, would not impair their position too drastically.[7] This

cautious optimism disappeared after Samuel had finished
reading his statement. 'Judas' and 'traitor' were words
which came to their lips. The sharpness of the Zionist
reaction to Samuel's speech was due as much to the general
apologetic and conciliatory tone of the speech as to the
'dangerous' interpretation he had, in their opinion, given to
the Balfour Declaration.[8]

Anxious to ease Arab fears of the 'unhappy misunderstanding' of the Declaration, Samuel gave his assurance that
the British Government had 'never consented and never will
consent . . . to their country, their holy places and their lands
being taken from them and given to strangers', and 'will
never agree to a Jewish Government being set up to rule over
the Moslem and Christian majority'. The real sense of the
Balfour Declaration, stated the High Commissioner, was
that 'the Jews, a people that are scattered throughout the
world, but whose hearts are always turned to Palestine,
should be enabled to found here [in Palestine] their home,
and some among them within the limits that are fixed by the
numbers and interests of the present population, should
come to Palestine in order to help develop the country by
their resources and efforts to the advantage of all the inhabitants'.[9]

The omission of the term 'national' from 'Home for the
Jewish people' and making the right of Jewish immigration
subordinate to the 'interests of the present population' were
interpreted by the Zionists as an attempt to obscure the
political weight of the Declaration and to diminish British
support of the Zionist cause.[10] The concrete implications of
this new approach for future immigration policy were, as
Samuel himself announced in his speech: first, that immigration should be 'strictly proportioned' to the employment
available in the country; second, that the enforcement of
immigration policy would remain exclusively in the hands of
the British authorities in Palestine and abroad; and finally
that nothing 'in the nature of a mass immigration' would be
permitted.

In his Statement, Samuel not only presented the general
principles of the new policy, but entered into details of the
method which would ensure adherence to these principles.

His scheme, which disregarded Morris's proposals, was based on the principle of classifying immigrants into various categories according to their professional make-up and their potential contribution to the economy of the country.

The idea of dividing immigrants into categories was not new, but rather an elaboration of the former method, outlined by Samuel himself and in force until May 1921. According to the old scheme, immigrants were divided into two main categories, 'A' — Zionists, persons coming under the auspices of the Zionist Organisation, and 'B' — persons other than Zionists. The latter category included those who were self-supporting and people able to obtain employment in Palestine, persons of religious occupation with sufficient means of maintenance and families of those at present resident in Palestine.[11] These groups formed the basis of Samuel's new scheme for seven separate and better-defined categories in the following order:

'A' — Travellers. Persons who do not intend to remain in Palestine for a period exceeding three months.

'B' — Persons of independent means who intend to take up permanent residence in Palestine.

'C' — Members of professions who intend to follow their calling.

'D' — Wives, children and other persons wholly dependent on residents of Palestine.

'E' — Persons who have a definite prospect of employment with specified employers or enterprises.

'F' — Persons of religious occupations, including the class of Jews who have come to Palestine in recent years from religious motives and who can show that they have means of maintenance here.

'G' — Returning residents.[12]

The most prominent change in the new system was the abolition of the former category 'A' — those who had come with the sanction of the Zionist Organisation, which consisted of over 80% of immigration prior to the suspension.[13] According to the new proposals, labour immigration, including those under the sanction of the Zionist Organisation, would be able to enter Palestine within category 'E', but only if they followed 'a particular specified trade and have a definite prospect of employment with specified employers or enterprises'. In this way, Samuel abolished the pool of labour schedules which had given the Zionists exclusive priority in selecting and regulating immigration, according to their own discretion.

The second significant change in Samuel's scheme was the enlargement of powers of control of the Department of Immigration and Travel in Jerusalem, at the expense of both the British Consuls and the Zionist Offices. Under the new scheme, it was necessary to refer to Jerusalem all applicants without independent means classified in the following categories: 'C' — members of professions, 'D' — persons dependent on residents of Palestine and 'E' — persons who had specific employment in Palestine. British Consuls were also requested to apply to Jerusalem in all irregular and doubtful cases before accepting or rejecting the applicant.[14]

On these points there was no real difference between Samuel's and Morris's schemes. Both intended to limit as far as possible dependence upon the Zionists and the British Consuls and to transfer the control over immigration from their hands to the Immigration Department in Jerusalem. It would seem, prima facie, that the only difference between the two systems was the question whether control over immigration should be carried out by permanent or current instructions from the Immigration Department, or by Immigration Officers subordinate to the Department but situated in Europe. However, this difference, in spite of its technical appearance, reveals an essential difference in attitude between Samuel and Morris to the entire question of immigration.

Morris, as head of the Immigration Department — a small and unimportant part of the Palestine Administration — was undoubtedly in favour of expanding its scope and activities. Being an administrative rather than a political personality, Morris was less sensitive than Samuel to the political implications of the immigration question. His proposal to place Immigration Officers in Europe was intended to improve control over immigration without necessarily limiting its extent. His scheme made it possible to come to a quick and correct decision on each case on the spot, allowing a smooth stream of immigration into Palestine.

Samuel, on the other hand, was more sensitive to the political effect of immigration, and the May Disturbances only served to increase his sensitivity. To prevent failure in control as had happened in the past, he insisted that immigration should now be controlled from Jerusalem. The division of immigrants into seven categories and frequent references to Jerusalem regarding a great number of the cases, made the method complicated and inflexible. Although aware of these deficiencies, Samuel did not seem to be particularly worried about the result of his policy, which was liable to reduce immigration significantly, as it suited his general 'gradualist' policy for the building up of the Jewish National Home. For this reason, Morris's proposal to set up a wide and expensive network of control in Europe became superfluous.

Shortly after he had finished outlining his scheme, Morris left on his mission to the Continent. It seems that at this stage his scheme had not reached the ears of either the Colonial Office or the Zionists. On the other hand, Samuel's scheme, as publicly announced in his Statement of 3rd June and approved post factum by Churchill,[15] was already in force by the end of May.[16]

ZIONIST CAMPAIGN IN LONDON: EFFORTS TO TURN BACK THE CLOCK

Zionist participation during the first stages of outlining the new immigration policy was, as we have seen, quite insignificant. This was a direct result of two main factors: the tension between Samuel and the Zionist Commission following the May Disturbances and the modest role delegated to the Zionist Organisation in the new scheme.

The Colonial Office, however, showed a different attitude to the future role of the Zionists in controlling immigration and a greater readiness to co-operate with them in elaborating a new policy. This attitude was due to good relations maintained with the Zionist Executive during and after the

May Disturbances, as well as to a certain disagreement with Samuel's behaviour during the Disturbances.[17] British goodwill was expressed not only in the frequent meetings between officials of the Colonial Office and members of the Zionist Executive during May and June, but also by British efforts regarding the deportation of immigrants to Europe.[18]

One may deduce with certainty that the efforts of the Colonial Office were intended to bring the 'tragic results' of the suspension of immigration to as speedy an end as possible and to come to a satisfactory agreement with the Zionists over the immigration question. Nevertheless, the impression remains that at this stage the Colonial Office was more anxious to reach an agreement over this question than the Zionists. This phenomenon might be explained by increasing sensitivity at the Colonial Office to public opinion and anti-Zionist criticism in Parliament of policy in Palestine. The Government was accused of placing a heavy and unnecessary financial burden on the 'British tax-payer' in order to keep up its Zionist policy, which appeared to be contrary to the wishes of the majority of the population of Palestine and whose moral value and contribution to the British interest were now called into question.[19] The anti-Zionist lobby in Parliament became stronger, particularly in the House of Lords, and was supported by newspaper 'tycoons' such as Lord Northcliffe and Lord Beaverbrook.[20]

As in Jerusalem in May and now in London, it was clear to all parties concerned that immigration policy was the root of the Palestine problem. As in the past, it was once more obvious that to obtain a solution to the political entanglement it was vital to settle the question of immigration. The search for such a solution was accelerated by the news of the impending arrival of the Palestine Arab Delegation to London.[21] It seems that Churchill wished to reach an agreement with the Zionists over the question of immigration before the arrival of the Delegation. An agreement such as this would have freed the Colonial Office from simultaneous negotiations with the Zionists and the Delegation. Failing this, Churchill suggested, it would be best for the two sides to meet and come to a 'working agreement' on this question. To this end, Churchill exerted much pressure on

Weizmann[22] and also on the Arab Delegation, soon after their arrival in London at the beginning of August.[23]

However, the Zionists were neither too enthusiastic at that moment over the idea of meeting the Arab Delegation nor over-anxious to arrive at an immediate solution to the immigration question. What they considered a more pressing priority was to halt what seemed to them "a dangerous process of deterioration" in the attitudes of the Administration and public opinion in Britain towards the realisation of the National Home.[24]

The only personality among the Zionist leaders competent enough to halt this process was Weizmann. It will be remembered that Weizmann had spent the critical period of May-June in the United States on a publicity and fund-raising campaign in connection with the opening of activities of the Keren Hayesod (Jewish Foundation Fund) in America.[25] The crisis which had overcome the American Zionist Movement at that time prevented his immediate return to London, in spite of urgent pleas from his colleagues to the effect that the 'whole political work of the last five years' depended upon his urgent presence in London.[26]

Weizmann returned to London at the beginning of July and began intensive contacts with prominent British political figures, as well as Colonial Office officials, bringing up the entire question of Palestine. His efforts were directed towards strengthening the traditional Zionist argument of the 'identity of interest' between Great Britain and Zionism, an argument which seemed to have been weakened by the aftermath of the May Disturbances. In this, he was helped by personal impressions of his recent visit to the United States. In his talks, he accentuated the strengthening and expansion of the Zionist idea among American Jewry and the current trend of anti-British feeling in American public opinion and Administration circles, which could lead to war between the two countries![27] The conclusion to be drawn from these two developments was clear — firm British support of the Zionist cause in Palestine would greatly improve Britain's image in the United States. Balfour was apparently impressed by Weizmann's arguments and suggested a meeting at his home with the Prime Minister and the Colonial Secretary at which Weizmann would be given the opportunity to voice his claims before a 'sympathetic circle'.[28]

The meeting, held on 22nd July, fulfilled those expectations. Weizmann was the main spokesman and his points received the full support of Lloyd George and Balfour, while Churchill, attempting to justify Samuel's policy in Palestine, placed himself in the minority. Weizmann began with his impressions of the United States and passed on to an analysis of the serious effects of Samuel's speech of 3rd June on the Zionist cause. In his opinion, the speech was contradictory to the Balfour Declaration, proposing an immigration policy which would absolutely prevent the creation of a Jewish majority in Palestine. Balfour and Lloyd George agreed with this, stating that 'by the Declaration they [had] always meant an eventual Jewish State'.[29]

Weizmann chose to give his arguments the form of a general protest, without suggesting concrete solutions to the various problems he had brought up, among them the question of immigration. But Churchill saw this latter point as a vital issue and pressed Weizmann to state 'what would satisfy him in the way of immigration?'. Weizmann was careful to mention neither numbers nor the method which in his opinion was suitable and avoided both these points by saying that, firstly, British support must be ensured for the economic development of Palestine, to make possible the smooth absorption of Jewish immigrants. Finally, it was agreed by all sides that they should strive towards finding practical solutions to the various questions raised at the meeting.[30]

Following this concession, Weizmann later met Churchill and discussed with him all the 'burning problems' in Palestine, such as approval of the Mandate; change of anti-Zionist officials in the Palestine Administration; the setting up of a Jewish police force; punishment of Arab rioters connected with the May Disturbances; approval of Rutenberg's electricity concessions for the development of industry and agriculture; and lastly, the question of immigration. On this matter Churchill undoubtedly shocked Weizmann, by suggesting that complete control of Jewish immigration into

Palestine be transferred to the Zionist Organisation. Weizmann rejected this proposal as 'not practical, so long as the Government of Palestine had the power to expel persons'. It seems that in reality, it was Weizmann's scepticism about the ability of the Zionist Organisation to control immigration efficiently which prevented him from accepting the proposal. Instead, he suggested that the control should remain in the hands of the British authorities, but that co-operation with the Zionist Organisation should be strengthened. Finally, Weizmann asked that 'immigration must be restricted for the time being'.[31]

Weizmann's objection to taking full control over immigration, and his demand to restrict it temporarily, represented the official policy of the Zionist Executive. This policy was presented in a confidential circular to the members of the Action Committee (the enlarged Zionist Executive) and to the Presidents of the Zionist Federations in August 1921, shortly before the 12th Zionist Congress. Referring to the suspension of immigration and Samuel's speech of 3rd June, the Executive explained the principles of its policy: 'The Executive has protested and will protest against these or any other restrictions placed upon Jewish immigrants on the part of the Government. At the same time the economic soundness of these [Samuel's] conditions, however unpleasant, cannot be contested.' The leaders of the Federations were surely surprised to discover the Zionist Executive's opposition even to the immediate departure of those who had been stranded in Europe, as a result of the suspension of immigration: 'We are well aware of the suffering, both moral and material, of the Halutzim (Jewish pioneers) in Warsaw, in Vienna and in Trieste. But it would be suicidal for us to transfer the unpleasant and degrading spectacle of our impotence in dealing with the Halutzim movement from Warsaw and Vienna to Jerusalem and Jaffa. The Executive must, therefore, state that while strongly protesting against the stoppage of immigration, it is compelled to emphasise that a sound influx óf immigrants can only proceed apace with the growth of the financial resources of the Zionist Organisation and the Keren Hayesod.'[32]

In the meantime, the Colonial Office had received further

details and explanations of Samuel's scheme, which they believed if 'generously construed', would satisfy the Zionists.[33] Churchill had since met Weizmann and tried to obtain his personal agreement to the new scheme, in order to enforce it as soon as possible. It seems that Weizmann agreed to the scheme, his only objection being the necessity for prior reference of each case recommended by the Zionist Organisation to Jerusalem. This reservation was accepted by Churchill, who asked Samuel to approve it.[34]

The extensive correspondence between the Colonial Office and the High Commissioner concerning this apparently trivial Zionist request shows up the differences in attitude, or rather the Colonial Office's misunderstanding of Samuel's new policy. Samuel saw in the proposed amendment a serious threat to this entire scheme, which intended to relieve the Zionist Offices in Europe of their privileged role in selection and regulation of immigration, particularly labour immigration. He therefore insisted that final authority in all cases coming under labour category 'E', must rest with the Palestine Administration.[35]

However, the Colonial Office considered this to be an inefficient and impractical system 'if the case of every one of the 100,000 immigrants whom it is hoped to introduce into Palestine in the course of the next three years' were to be referred back.[36] This estimate of immigration to come indicates more than anything else the significantly different views of the Zionist Organisation and the Colonial Office on the one hand and Samuel's gradualist policy on the other.[37]

The Zionist cause received support from an unexpected source with the arrival of Major Morris in London, at the beginning of September. Morris strengthened the Colonial Office's case in favour of 'giving the Zionist Organisation the right to settle immigrants to whom they can guarantee employment without the necessity for referring each individual case to the High Commissioner'.[38] In Morris's opinion it was 'obvious that immigration is the foundation on which the National Home must be built up, so it is to the interest of the Palestine Government that immigrants who are allowed to enter Palestine should be the best possible immigrants that can be found . . .'[39]

Samuel finally gave in to pressure from London on this issue and agreed that the Colonial Office should continue contacts with the Zionists and arrive at a working agreement concerning the new scheme.[40] Nevertheless, negotiations were postponed until the return of Weizmann and Sokolow to London, as Colonial Office officials had 'a very little confidence in the other members of the Executive to take the broad and sensible view which this matter requires'.[41]

Despite the views which Morris expressed at the Colonial Office while visiting London, the findings in his report written a few months earlier, regarding the failure of the Zionists to control immigration, caused the Colonial Office to re-examine its stand on the intended role of the Zionists on control of immigration. British flexibility and understanding of the Zionists' demands gave way to disappointment and impatience when the Zionists would not 'come and put all their cards on the table'. Pending talks with the Zionists it was decided to re-examine the whole question on the basis of the Morris Report and prepare points for discussion.[42]

The Colonial Office's re-examination did not change its basic concept regarding the Zionists' role in control of immigration. However, this now depended upon whether the Zionists would succeed in persuading their British colleagues that past oversights would not be repeated. The Colonial Office therefore requested to know how the Zionist Organisation would ensure that the selected immigrants would be politically and socially suitable as settlers, and technically and physically qualified for their destined jobs in Palestine.[43] If satisfactory answers could be given to those questions it was proposed to give the Zionist Organisation a trial period; but if the mistakes of the past recurred it would be necessary 'to take control out of their hands' and appoint British Immigration Officers to do that 'job'.[44]

The Morris Report, which caused the Colonial Office to re-examine its attitude to the immigration question, also stimulated the Zionist Executive into action. Information regarding the existence of the Report, and on the severe criticism levelled against the Zionist Organisation, worried the Zionist Executive in London. The Executive requested its people in Jerusalem to send them the Report urgently, but

Morris continually postponed sending the Report to the Zionist Commission and finally left for London without letting them have it. Jerusalem suggested instead that the Executive should forward its comments to the Colonial Office in some unofficial manner, 'to rectify the bad impression which may have been created by the Report'.[45] However, the Zionists in Jerusalem apparently succeeded in obtaining a copy of the Report and sent it urgently to London.[46] Thus while Colonial Office officials were outlining their policy on the basis of the Report's findings and having personal consultations with Major Morris, officials of the Zionist Executive in the offices at Great Russell Street, were preparing their own comments on the Report. It seems that the Executive was firm in its opinion that there was no point in entering into concrete discussions on the question of immigration before being given an opportunity to present their own interpretation on the subjects with which Morris had dealt in his Report.

The apologetic and controversial nature of the Zionists' comments on the Morris Report certainly made it more difficult to obtain a clear picture of their opinion regarding future control of immigration. But in actual fact their observations were not intended to give such a picture, but rather to contradict Morris's findings. Yet it is not difficult to deduce from the Zionists' memorandum that they were attempting to renew the previous system of control. In their defence, the Zionists pointed out that the old method had been in use for only a very short period and that some time was required to enable their Offices to adapt themselves to the Regulations; that the cautious policy of the Executive had itself reduced the number of Zionist guaranteed immigrants from 16,500 families to 2,300 persons; and that the Consuls had full responsibility for 'non-guaranteed' immigrants, a fact which Morris had completely disregarded in his Report.[47]

Nevertheless, the Executive did admit that there had been shortcomings in the Zionist control, which were caused by the financial dependence of the Palestine Offices on the local Zionist Federations. The natural tendency of the Federations to promote the Zionist cause among their people by sensational propaganda in favour of immigration to Palestine, militated against control on the part of the Executive over the Palestine Offices. In order to rectify this situation, the Executive decided that they should take over the budget and with it the direct supervision of the Palestine Offices 'in order to bring their activities more into line with the actual requirements of Palestine'.[48]

In the meantime John Shuckburgh, head of the Middle East Department, had confidentially sent Weizmann the Colonial Office memorandum, which was based on the findings of the Morris Report. He invited him to arrange a meeting as soon as possible, to deal with several questions in order to formulate revised instructions to be sent to the British Consuls.[49] Weizmann replied at once, but avoided mention of a date for the requested meeting.[50] It appears that the Colonial Office's memorandum not only did not advance negotiations with the Zionists but, on the contrary, held them back a further three weeks, in which time the Executive was able to prepare a new memorandum in reply to that of the Colonial Office. It seems that this time Weizmann had personally taken part in the memorandum's preparation. This document took the form of a review of immigration policy since the setting-up of the Civil Administration in Palestine. Its main purpose was to strengthen the confidence of the British Government in the ability of the Zionist Organisation to maintain efficient and responsible control over labour immigration to Palestine and to demand more vigorously that this authority should not be taken away from them. With an assurance not to exceed the agreed number and that the entry of 'undesirable' elements into Palestine would be prevented, the Zionists pressed for restoration of the old scheme of 'agreeable quota for guaranteed immigrants'. Their moderate estimate of labour immigrants required for the the two coming years (25,000), and their undertaking that one third of this number would consist of skilled labour, illustrate the Zionists' wish to satisfy the British.[51]

Regarding 'non-guaranteed' immigrants, the Zionists agreed with Samuel's proposals that they 'should be dealt with on their merits without any general limit of numbers'.

Nevertheless, the Executive insisted on omitting the condition that 'non-guaranteed' immigrants coming under Category 'E' (labour) should have a definite prospect of employment with specified employers or enterprises, describing this condition as 'unworkable in practice' and 'unparalleled in immigration laws enforced elsewhere'. Generally, Palestine immigration laws should not be stricter than those of any other countries.[52]

It seems that the Executive's tactics achieved even more positive results than anticipated, causing internal dissension and confusion among the Zionists themselves. At the conference on the question of immigration which finally took place on 25th November, Weizmann succeeded in dispelling the doubts of the Colonial Office officials and gaining their full confidence in the ability of the Zionists to control immigration 'even more admirably than any other Government'. As with the whole Palestine question, Weizmann endeavoured to accentuate the British and Zionist identity of interests now apparent in the common wish to prevent the entry of politically undesirable elements. To this end, he offered the help of the Zionist Organisation in recommending and selecting the 'non-guaranteed' immigrants as well as the 'guaranteed'.[53]

The only opposition to this offer surprisingly came from the Zionist side. Leonard Stein, the Political Secretary, rejected the idea that all Jewish immigrants should be obliged to obtain a reference from the Zionist Organisation, 'a system which would rule out all possibilities of immigration to a Jew who was disliked by the local Zionist Organisation'. But the British accepted Weizmann's offer, stating that 'however unfortunate this might be, it was desirable to protect the Palestine Government as much as is possible . . . from the introduction of undesirable immigrants'.[54]

A similar episode occurred during the proceedings when Weizmann suggested (and officials of the Colonial Office agreed with him) that Immigration Officers should be 'travelling inspectors', whose duties would chiefly be to check immigrants against records supplied by the Zionist Organisation. Stein, on the other hand, was in favour of Morris's recommendation to appoint Immigration Officers in certain European centres, who would combine all functions of the British Consuls and the local Zionist Offices. Although there was 'no definite crystallisation of opinion', as G.M. Clauson remarked in his minutes, 'generally, the Conference agreed with Dr. Weizmann'.

Weizmann undoubtedly played a major part in obtaining the agreement of the Colonial Office to the Zionists' proposals. His success was due to his ability to pinpoint the main fear of the British Administration — the danger of infiltration to Palestine by politically undesirable elements who could cause agitation and unrest — and to offer the Zionists' help on this matter.

Acceptance of the Zionists' offer inevitably necessitated the expansion of their authority to recommend and select all Jewish immigrants to Palestine, in fact, more than the Zionists were actually ready to take upon themselves. Stein apparently succeeded in persuading Weizmann to revoke his offer that recommendation for Jewish 'non-guaranteed' immigrants should be dealt with by the Colonial Office. Writing to the Colonial Office, Weizmann explained that this 'privilege' would impose a corresponding obligation upon the Zionist Organisation, which would have to 'morally assume full responsibility for all Jewish immigrants', and would expose the Organisation to 'constant criticism' and 'complaints of favouritism and of discrimination on personal or political grounds'. Instead, he suggested leaving complete control over 'non-guaranteed' immigrants in the hands of British Consuls and the Palestine Administration.[55] This shows the Executive's intention of concentrating particularly on labour immigration for the time being, disregarding middle class and 'unorganised' immigration. But in spite of the Zionists' unpretentious stand, the Colonial Office was still of the opinion that Zionist recommendation for all Jewish immigration to Palestine was vital, to ensure sufficient control.

In retrospect, however, there was no reason to overestimate the Zionist achievement. Indeed, the provisional agreement with the Colonial Office ensured co-operation with the Zionists in controlling immigration, but it also endorsed Samuel's entire scheme. Its rigid and bureaucratic nature enabled the Administration to intervene frequently, particularly in regard to the 'non-guaranteed' immigrants. This, the Zionists' undertaking to include 'skilled labour' in the schedules of 'guaranteed' immigrants, and the necessity to re-approve the schedule every three months, became the main causes of friction between the Palestine Zionist Executive and the Palestine Administration in the coming years.

TOWARDS A 'WORKING AGREEMENT'

Samuel's Statement of 3rd June officially ended the preliminary formation of the revised policy in Palestine. The second stage began with Churchill's Statement in the House of Commons on 14th June. The political centre of gravity shifted from Jerusalem to London for the whole of the coming year.

Describing most sympathetically the Zionists' achievements in Palestine, the Colonial Secretary firmly insisted on Britain's responsibility towards fulfilling the Balfour Declaration. Churchill assured Parliament that Jewish immigration into Palestine had hitherto been 'very carefully watched and controlled' and saw 'no reason why with care and progress there, there should not be a steady flow of Jewish immigration . . . accompanied at every stage by a general increase in the wealth of the whole of the existing population . . .' But, unlike Samuel, he was not afraid to pinpoint the conflicting Arab and Jewish demands focused on that question. Acceptance of Arab demands for representative institutions, stated the Secretary of State, 'would certainly veto all further Jewish immigration' and this could not happen 'without definitely accepting the position that the word of Britain no longer counts in the East . . .' Therefore, if these institutions were to be conceded, 'some definite arrangements' would have to be made to safeguard Jewish rights to come to Palestine.[56] On these lines, the Colonial Office intended to conduct its talks with the Arab Delegation which was expected in London at the beginning of August.[57]

The Delegation was not encouraged by the British to come to London, nor was it recognised as a representative body of the Palestinian Arab population. However, opinion in Jerusalem and London was that, since the Delegation had already come to London, advantage should be taken of its presence to reach an agreement over the political questions of Palestine.[58] At their first meeting, Churchill had insisted that the Delegation should meet Weizmann, if not officially, then privately, and that they should together try to come to 'some form of working agreement' over the immigration question. Churchill suggested that the agreement could be based on a prior fixed number of immigrants to be allowed to come to Palestine 'year by year for the next five years'. In this way, it would be possible to ease Arab fears of being 'floated by alien immigrants' and at the same time ensure that a certain number of Jews were allowed to come to Palestine in order to develop their National Home.[59]

In contrast with the pragmatic approach of the British, the Arab Delegation came to London furnished with far-reaching national demands. These were not new, and included the abolition of the idea of a Jewish National Home; creation of a 'National Government' in Palestine, responsible to an elected Parliament; and the stoppage of Jewish immigration, until the time when such a Government was formed.[60] The Delegation rejected the idea of meeting Dr. Weizmann or any other Zionist personality at the outset, stating that they did not recognise the Zionist Organisation and that their instructions were to negotiate with the British Government and not with the Zionists. 'We like our argument to be with the Government', explained Musa Kazim Pasha, the President of the Delegation, 'because it has the power that can give or take away from us'. At this meeting, and at the following one ten days later, Churchill repeated his appeal for a less uncompromising and more flexible attitude from the Delegation towards a practical agreement on the political questions. Speaking to them 'plainly and in blunt terms' he characterised their demands for a National Government and for the abolition of the Balfour Declaration as non-discussable and tried to convince them that their only political outlet was to co-operate with the Government by reaching an agreement which, even 'if it did not give them control, it would give them influence'.[61]

The effectiveness of this 'influence' had to depend upon the extent of power granted to the Palestine population through the proposed representative institutions. After two fruitless meetings with the Secretary of State, the Delegation was informed of the proposed schemes for these institutions. Major Young submitted to them four alternative schemes for a Legislative Assembly. These alternatives were based on various combinations of two different prototypes: either an 'advisory assembly on an entirely elective basis with no legislative power' or a 'legislative assembly with a permanent majority of officials or nominated members, to ensure the due carrying out of the policy of His Majesty's Government'.[62] The last condition was mainly directed at the power to control Jewish immigration.

The Delegation rejected all British proposals, stating that none of the proposed bodies gave 'truly representative character' and 'power to control over the Executive' to 'the hands of the people'.[63] Instead they submitted their own constitutional plan which recommended the granting of executive powers to a 'representative Government, giving the inhabitants control over their domestic affairs, but acting with the advice of the helping power'. The control of immigration, regarded as a 'domestic affair', was left 'in the hands of the people of Palestine'. The immigration policy, emphasised the Delegation, 'should be regulated not in the interests of the Zionists, but of the Palestinians'.[64]

The rejection of the British proposals put the talks with the Delegation at a deadlock. The Colonial Office gave the Arabs to understand that in its opinion the continuation of negotiations was pointless.[65] Colonial Office officials believed that the uncompromising attitude of the Arabs was derived from their feeling of being 'discredited in Palestine', and that 'if any one of them weakens, the remainder will attach to him all ignominy when they return to Palestine'. This internal suspicion between the members of the Delegation, their inability to express themselves in English and their being 'very slow of understanding' made the Delegation, in the opinion of the British, 'a hopeless body to deal with'.[66]

The conclusion of the Colonial Office on the situation was 'that the time has come to leave off arguing and announce plainly and authoritatively what the Government proposes to do'. Being 'orientals', presumed Shuckburgh, the Arabs 'will understand an order and if once they realise that we [the British] mean business, may be expected to acquiesce'. Accordingly, he suggested, the Secretary of State should invite the Arab Delegation and representatives of the Zionist Organisation to a joint conference at the Colonial Office, for the purpose of making a statement on future policy in Palestine.[67] This would either set the negotiations on more concrete lines or end them absolutely. Shuckburgh invited the Arab Delegation to a joint meeting with the Secretary of State and the Zionists, thus giving the Delegation to understand that the meeting was a direct result of their uncompromising stand.[68] Apparently, the Colonial Office changed its mind and cancelled the proposed meeting.[69] There is no evidence of any pressure coming from the Delegation to bring about this cancellation, but it doubtless served the Arabs' cause well by preventing the immediate termination of negotiations.[70]

It seems, however, that the Colonial Office's rigid stance forced the Delegation into accepting the idea of meeting representatives of the Zionist Organisation, as the lesser of two evils. Over a luncheon with the Secretary of State on 25th November, the Delegation agreed to meet Weizmann for 'an informal exchange of views', apparently believing that this was a condition of a favourable agreement with the Government.[71] At any rate, this was the reason which they later on gave for accepting Churchill's request. Whatever the later explanations were to be, the Delegation was undoubtedly anxious to renew talks with the British, as they hoped to bring about a radical change in British policy in Palestine.[72]

A remark made by Musa Kazim at the aforementioned luncheon about 'no objection to Jewish immigration itself, so long as it did not outrun the capacity of the country to absorb it',[73] and the successful conference that same day with the Zionists on immigration,[74] might have aroused some British hope of arriving at a working agreement on this question. But the Arab-Zionist meeting which finally took place on 29th November could not have been further from fulfilling these hopes.

Endeavouring to bridge the gap between the two parties, Shuckburgh, the chairman, assumed a general acceptance of several propositions of 'a non-controversial nature' as an indication that there were 'common grounds' for reaching an agreement.[75] But by his introduction of topics such as 'the real fear with which the Arabs regarded the idea of Jewish immigration' and 'the contingency of Jewish political ascendency in Palestine', the discussion turned into a controversial and impractical argument.

This gave the two parties the opportunity of making political statements which showed their irreconcilable stands. Dr. Weizmann, making a 'conciliatory speech', appealed for co-operation between the 'two nations' in the upbuilding of Palestine and invited the Delegation to enter into immediate concrete discussions. Musa Kazim Pasha, on the other hand, rejected any 'discussion' or 'understanding' with people whom he considered as 'aggressors' — at any rate, if such a discussion had to be based on Arab acceptance of the Balfour Declaration. Discussing the various interpretations of the Declaration, Musa Kazim made it a condition that a new official interpretation of the Declaration should be made if the Delegation was to participate in further negotiations. To prevent the complete failure of the Conference, Shuckburgh agreed to prepare a new 'formula' for the Declaration.

The failure of the meeting illustrated the slim chances of bringing the two parties to a 'working agreement' without making a significant change in the entire Palestine policy.[76] By re-interpreting the Balfour Declaration the Colonial Office did not intend to make such a change but merely a new verbal 'basis of negotiations' between the two parties. Shuckburgh, who took it upon himself to draw up a new formula, was quite sceptical about the effectiveness of his own proposal. But in his opinion there was no need for hurry to reach the next stage, and even perhaps some advantage in allowing the parties 'to kick their heels a little'.[77]

Weizmann, on the other hand, could not remain indifferent to this latest move of the Colonial Office and expressed his fears that the proposed re-interpretation 'would at once weaken very seriously the bargaining power of the Zionist Organisation', and furthermore 'it could only have the effect of greatly impairing any prospects there may be of a working agreement on issues of practical importance'.[78]

The Zionist fears of a new interpretation of the Balfour Declaration — their principal recognised legitimate foothold in Palestine — were natural and sincere, but their desire to reach a 'working agreement' with the Arabs on the immigration question deserves further consideration. Obviously, the Zionists were interested in reaching an agreement with the Arabs, in order to remove all possible obstacles in the way of their activities in Palestine. How far they were really ready to go towards the Arab demands is quite impossible to judge, even after their joint meeting, since their readiness to compromise was not brought to the test by the Arabs.

The results nevertheless remained more concrete and meaningful from the Zionists' point of view. Their success in obtaining the confidence of the Colonial Office over control of immigration, as agreed at their joint meeting a few days previously,[79] made the proposed agreement with the Arab Delegation if not unnecessary, then of secondary importance. Although there is no reason to conclude that the British-Zionist Conference on immigration directly damaged the prospects of an Arab-Zionist agreement, nevertheless the success of the first and the failure of the latter had a very significant effect on future immigration policy.

Returning to our topic, one might say that the failure of the Arab-Zionist meeting placed the British-Arab negotiations in a new deadlock. Shuckburgh kept his promise, although after a long delay, and sent the Delegation a new formula for the Balfour Declaration. The re-interpretation was, as expected, rejected by the Arabs, who protested against the formula's recognition of 'historic and religious associations that connected the Jewish people with Palestine'. Opposing this connection, the Delegation could not find any reason for 'special facilities' for Jewish immigration into Palestine. The Delegation also rejected the principle of Economic Absorptive Capacity of the country as unjust and irrelevant, stating that 'even supposing that Palestine is economically unaffected by Jewish immigrants there can be no doubt as to the political harm that their presence must threaten Arab interests'.[80] A week later, the Delegation re-applied to the Colonial Office requesting that 'it is only right and fair' that while they were negotiating with the Government, Jewish immigration to Palestine should be stopped.[81]

The re-focusing of Arab demands on the immigration question spurred the Colonial Office on once more to find an 'urgent solution' to the question. In spite of the Colonial Office decision to suspend all further contacts with the Delegation, following a suspicion that they had communicated to the *Morning Post* the draft constitution of Palestine (in defiance of the Secretary of State's injunction that it was to be treated confidentially),[82] Colonial Office officials took urgent steps to find such a solution. Their proposal suggested setting up an Immigration Board, quite irrespective of the Palestine constitution and without considering Jewish or Arab demands.[83] It was further recommended that the proposed body should be 'representative of Palestinians of all classes' and would advise the High Commissioner on immigration questions 'from the point of view of the inhabitants of Palestine'. At the same time, the Palestine Zionist Executive would advise the High Commissioner from its particular point of view. In the event of an irreconcilable difference of opinion the points at issue would be referred to London for decision.[84]

It seems that Colonial Office officials were inclined to believe that by isolating and solving separately the question of immigration, they might succeed in advancing the negotiations with the Arab Delegation on the question of the proposed constitution of Palestine. The fact that Dr. Eder of the Palestine Zionist Executive, at the time in London, 'was not altogether unfavourable' to that proposal, encouraged them to act without any further delay.[85] Without waiting for Samuel's approval, the Colonial Office tackled the immigration question 'promptly' and sent their proposals to the Arab Delegation.[86] In this way they reversed their ban on further communications with the Arabs, and started a new round of talks.

It seems that the Delegation did not give serious considera- tion to the new British proposals, objecting that the Zionist Organisation should also have 'a point of view' and that 'the capacity of the proposed board will be in effect consultative'. They insisted on their old conception that 'the best safeguard is the creation of a National Government which will consider the question of immigration in so far as it is compatible with the interests and capacity of the country'.[87]

Meanwhile, Samuel's reply to the proposals of the Colonial Office had reached London. Samuel had succeeded in anticipating the Arab reaction much better, stating that the transfer of control of immigration from the proposed elected body to 'nominees of the Government' would be attributed to 'Zionist motives'. In spite of that, he suggested that a 'standing committee' from the proposed Legislative Council be appointed to consist of half the total number of elected representatives, and with purely 'critical and advisory' functions.[88] Samuel's revision compelled the Colonial Office to appeal once more to the Delegation with a more acceptable version of the proposed Board. But all this was in vain. The Colonial Office again came to the conclusion that there was no prospect whatsoever of moving the Delegation from its obstinate stand and that sooner or later the British would have to give the 'last word'. Nevertheless, it was decided in London to consider the request of the Palestine Administration and to 'keep the Delegation in play', at any rate until after Easter, in order to avoid any risk of disturbances in Palestine.[89]

With the failure of this last attempt on April 22nd, the Colonial Office returned to its old plan of November 1921 — to make a statement regarding policy in Palestine, which would inevitably end the present negotiations with the Arab Delegation. The intention of the Colonial Office was to collect together Samuel's speech of 3rd June, Churchill's statement of 14th June and selected correspondence of the Colonial Office with the Arab Delegation and the Zionist Executive during the previous year, in the form of a White Paper on British policy in Palestine. For this reason, Samuel was asked to bring forward his proposed visit to London and, with the co-operation of the Middle East Department of the Colonial Office, to draft a new statement of policy.[90]

The Statement, a new official interpretation of the Balfour Declaration, rigorously set aside any 'exaggerated interpretation' of the Declaration, affirming that His Majesty's Government had never had the intention of making Palestine 'as Jewish as England is English' or that 'Palestine as a whole should be converted into a Jewish National Home', while the idea was, in fact, that 'such a Home should be founded *in Palestine*'.[91] By recognising the connection between the Jewish people and Palestine as 'ancient historic connections' the Statement determined the presence of the Jews in Palestine to be 'as of right and not on sufferance'.

Turning to the immigration policy, the Statement declared that 'it is necessary that the Jewish Community in Palestine should be able to increase its numbers by immigration'. But this immigration should not be so great in volume 'as to exceed whatever may be the economic capacity of the country at the time to absorb new arrivals'. This gave official approval to the leading principle of the new immigration policy, better known as the principle of Economic Absorptive Capacity.

In this 'new' principle, there was, in fact, nothing new. Major General Bols, the Military Chief Administrator in Palestine, had already announced it in April 1920, when he gave the first official interpretation of the Balfour Declaration.[92] Since then Samuel and Churchill had repeated this principle, although in different verbal versions on various occasions.[93]

By accepting the White Paper as a whole, the Zionist Organisation endorsed this principle and expressed its confidence that both His Majesty's Government and the Administration of Palestine would be guided by this principle and would not deviate from it. In other words, they trusted that political pressure, disturbances or any other factors would not influence immigration policy, as had been the case in the past.[94] Although the Zionists did not regard the White Paper as a great triumph, but rather as a 'necessary condition' for the confirmation of the Mandate by the League of Nations, this principle was not in contradiction with their policy. Weizmann and other members of the Executive believed that if this policy were carried out 'honestly and conscientiously' it would still afford the Zionists a framework for building up a Jewish majority in Palestine and for the eventual emergence of a 'Jewish State'. Yet, 'absorptive capacity' had still to be created and this remained the major task of the Zionist Organisation.[95]

The Arab Delegation, which had already explained the irrelevance of the economic factor as an exclusive indicator for immigration policy, claimed in its reply that hitherto even this principle had not been adhered to, the proof being the 'turning out' of Arabs from their jobs and the prevailing grave unemployment in Palestine. But pointing out the political and social effects of 'immigration of a foreign element' on the 'native population' of the country, the Delegation repeated its demand for the creation of a 'Representative National Government, which shall have complete control of immigration'.[96] The Delegation rejected the White Paper, which did not satisfy this demand.

Despite the rejection of the White Paper by the House of Lords, Churchill succeeded in gaining a decisive majority on Government policy in Palestine in the House of Commons. This and the ratification of the Palestine Mandate by the League of Nations later in July brought to an end the political campaign for Palestine in London and shifted it back to its original centre.

NOTES

[1] Albert M. Hyamson, Department of Immigration and Travel, Jerusalem, to Samuel Landman, General Secretary of the Zionist Organisation, London, in a semi-official letter, 8.5.21, I.S.A. 11/2/1.
[2] Samuel to C.O., Despatch 82 confidential, 8.5.21, C.O.733/3 file 24660.
[3] 'Memorandum on Immigration into Palestine', Department of Immigration and Travel, 30.5.21, I.S.A. 11/3.
[4] Ibid, ibid.
[5] Ibid, ibid.
[6] Eder to Z.E., reporting on his interview with the High Comissioner on 31.5.21, 'confidential', 4.6.21, C.Z.A. Z4/16151.
[7] Ibid, ibid. This long letter, which was written at various intervals during

the week before and after Samuel's speech, gives an interesting observation of some of the Zionists' 'expectations' and 'disappointments'.

[8] Ibid, ibid; Ruppin, *Memoirs,* p.191.

[9] See Samuel's speech of 3rd June enclosed in Despatch 139 to C.O., 6.6.21, C.O.733/3 file 30263.

[10] For a comprehensive discussion of this see Caplan, *The Yishuv,* pp. 174-84; also Friesel, *Weizmann's First Steps,* pp. 262-3; Attias, *Sefer Ha-Teudot,* pp.63f. Porath, *The Emergence,* pp. 132-3.

[11] See 'Instruction to Consuls Regarding Granting of Visas' Appendix 2.

[12] Samuel to Churchill, Despatch 227, 16.7.21, C.O.733/4 file 37860.

[13] 9,191 immigrants with Zionist Commission guarantee, out of total of 10,652 immigrants. Appendix 5.

[14] See note 12 above.

[15] Churchill to Samuel, tel.122, 2.6.21, C.O.733/3 file 26711.

[16] Samuel to Churchill, tel. 177, 24.5.21, I.S.A. 11/3.

[17] See notes of interview of J. Cowen and S. Landman of Z.E. with Churchill, 9.5.21, 'confidential', C.Z.A. Z4/302/4A; 'Notes of conversation at the Colonial Office', 14.5.21, 'confidential', ibid; Richard Lichtheim, member of Z.E. to Weizmann, 24.5.21, C.Z.A., Z4/305/9; Weizmann to Schmarya Levin, member of Zionist Executive 15.7.21, W.A.; Meinertzhagen, *Middle East Diaries,* pp. 101-2.

[18] See Chapter 2 pp. 27-8.

[19] See 'Notes of Conversation at the Colonial Office', 14.5.21, 'confidential', C.Z.A. Z4/302/4A.

[20] Weizmann, *Trial,* p. 349.

[21] See 'Moslem-Christian Delegation to Europe', a memo by John Shuckburgh, head of Middle East Dept., at the C.O., 23.7.21, C.O.733/13 file 37529; 'Palestine' memo submitted to the Cabinet by Sec. of State for Colonies 11.8.21, CAB. 24/127.

[22] See 'Notes of conversation held at Mr. Balfour's house . . .' on 22.7.21; Meinertzhagen, *Middle East,* pp. 103-6; minutes of Z.E. meeting 3.8.21., C.Z.A. Z4/302/4A.

[23] See note 24 below.

[24] Weizmann to his wife Vera, 14.8.21, W.A.; during conversation at Balfour's house (see note 22 above), Weizmann considered the Arabs as 'political blackmailers' and said that he could only talk to them when he knew the position of the British Government.

[25] Weizmann, *Trial,* pp. 333-42; Friesel, *Weizmann*, pp.236-56.

[26] Z.E. London, to Weizmann, New York, 14.5.21, C.Z.A., L3/31; Eder to Weizmann, 6.5.21, ibid, Z4/305/9.

[27] Weizmann to Balfour, 6.7.21, W.A.; Meinertzhagen, *Middle East,* pp. 100-101.

[28] Friesel, Weizmann, pp. 263-4.

[29] 'Note of conversation', see note 22 above.

[30] For Weizmann's impression of that conversation see Weizmann to Achad Ha'am, the well-known Zionist thinker 30.7.21, W.A.; Weizmann to Wyndham Deedes, Chief Secretary of Palestine, 31.7.21, ibid; Weizmann to Shuckburgh 'private and personal', 16.11.21, C.Z.A.

Z4/16055; for impression at Colonial Office see 'minutes of covering letter' by Shuckburgh to his memo 'Political Situation in Palestine', 7.11.21, C.O.733/15 file 57572.

[31] This meeting was mainly based on topics of the Z.O. memo submitted to Churchill on 21.7.21, one day before the meeting at Balfour's house, see memo in C.O.733/16 file 38128; see also Weizmann's report of the meeting with the Secretary of State in minutes of Z.E. meeting on 3.8.21, C.Z.A. Z4/302/4A.

[32] 'The Jaffa Events' — circular letter to members of the Action Committee and Presidents of Federations, July 1921, W.A.

[33] See Samuel's proposals in Despatch 227, 16.7.21, and minutes by Richard Meinertzhagen, then Military Adviser of Middle East Department, C.O., 3.8.21, both in C.O.733/4 file 37860.

[34] Churchill to Samuel, tel. 251, 30.8.21, C.O.733/4, file 37860; in this meeting Weizmann submitted to the Colonial Office an additional memo: 'Memorandum on the new phases of Jewish activities in Palestine', see also minutes by Major Young of the Colonial Office regarding this memo, 17.8.21, both in C.O.733/4 file 41795.

[35] Samuel to Churchill, tel. 360, 5.9.21, C.O.733/6 file 44737.

[36] Gerald L.M. Clauson of Middle East Department, C.O. minutes, 6.9.21, ibid.

[37] During those three years less than 30,000 Jews immigrated to Palestine, but only about half of them came under the guarantee of the Zionist Organisation, see Appendices 6 and 7.

[38] See note 36 above.

[39] G.L.M. Clauson, minutes, 7.10.21, C.O.733/6, file 49714.

[40] Samuel to Churchill, tel. 381, 21.9.21; see Clauson's minutes on Samuel's reply 23.9.21, both in C.O.733/6 file 47443; Samuel to Churchill 4.10.21, tel 405, 4.10.21, C.O.733/6 file 49714.

[41] Clauson's minutes, 7.10.21, ibid.

[42] Shuckburgh to Clauson, minutes, 12.10.21, ibid.

[43] See 'Memorandum on Jewish immigration into Palestine', 19.10.21, ibid; also in I.S.A. 11/6, prepared by Clauson and S.M. Campbell; see Shuckburgh in minutes to Sir James E. Masterton-Smith, Permanent Under-Secretary of State for the Colonies, 20.10.21, C.O.733/6 file 47914.

[44] Clauson in minutes, 7.10.21, ibid.

[45] Dr. M. Eliash of Z.C. Jerusalem, to Leonard Stein, Politcal Secretary of Zionist Organisation, London, 18.9.21, C.Z.A. S6/296.

[46] Stein to Eliash, 6.10.21, ibid.

[47] 'Comment on the Report of Major Morris . . .' 29.10.21, C.Z.A., S6/272. The 'comments' were most probably written by L. Stein, see note 45 above.

[48] Ibid, ibid.

[49] Shuckburgh to Weizmann, 1.11.21, C.O.733/6 file 49714.

[50] Weizmann to Shuckburgh, 2.11.21, ibid.

[51] Weizmann to Shuckburgh in attached letter to memo dated 22.11.21.; Weizmann's signature appears on memo entitled ''Jewish immigration

into Palestine'' which is 60 pages long and includes 15 appendices, C.O.733/16 file 58538.

[52] See 'proposals' of the memo pp. 20-3, ibid.

[53] Ibid,ibid.

[54] See notes of the conference, C.O.733/16 file 58536, also in I.S.A. 11/6; see minutes of Z.E. meeting 24.11.21, C.Z.A., Z4/302/6.

[55] Weizmann to Shuckburgh, 7.12.21, C.O.733/16 file 58533.

[56] See text of Churchill's speech in the House of Commons on British policy in the Middle East, 14.6.21, C.O.733/7 file 57955.

[57] 'Moslem-Christian Delegation to Europe', Shuckburgh's memo, 23.7.21, C.O.733/13 file 37529.

[58] Ibid, ibid; interview of members of the Delegation with Samuel, 23.6.21, C.O.733/4 file 33632; notes of interview of representatives of Zionist Executive with Major Young 23.8.21, W.A.; Young's minutes to Churchill, 22.8.21, C.O.733/14 file 42762; Shuckburgh's minutes, 29.9.21, C.O.733/6 file 48808.

[59] Report of conversation between Churchill and the Arab Delegation, 12.8.21, C.O.733/17b file 41298; notes of conversation of Major Young with the Delegation, 11.8.21, C.O.733/14 file 40713.

[60] See 'A brief Statement of the Demands . . .' of the Arab Delegation submitted to the Secretary of State for the Colonies, 12.8.21, C.O.733/14 file 42635.

[61] Note 59 above; notes of conversation with the Delegation, 22.8.21, C.O.733/14 file 42762.

[62] Notes of Conversation . . . 23.8.21, C.O.733/14. On the same day Major Young also met representatives of the Z.E. and reported to them on his meeting with the Delegation, see note 58; see also 'Notes of Conference of Legal Advisers . . . Constitution of Palestine', 12-13.8.21, C.O.733/14 file 42532.

[63] The Palestine Arab Delegation to Churchill, 1.9.21, C.O.733/16 file 44017.

[64] The Palestine Arab Delegation to Churchill, 24.10.21, C.O.733/16 file 53080.

[65] Shuckburgh at a meeting with the.Delegation, 15.9.21, C.O.733/15 file 46936; Shuckburgh's minutes, 29.9.21, C.O.733/6 file 48808.

[66] 'Political Situation in Palestine' a memo by Shuckburgh 7.11.21, C.O.733/15 file 57572; Comments by Eric Mills, Middle East Department, C.O., 30.11.21, C.O.537/855.

[67] Shuckburgh's memo; 7.11.21, ibid.

[68] Shuckburgh to the Delegation, 12.11.21, C.O.733/16 file 53080.

[69] Weizmann to Wyndham Deedes, 13.12.21, C.O.537/854.

[70] Arab Delegation in a meeting with Shuckburgh, 15.9.21, see note 65 above.

[71] 'The twenty-first despatch', 16.12.21, Porath, *Emergence,* p. 65.

[72] The Delegation to Churchill, 24.10.21, C.O.733/16 file 53080.

[73] Shuckburgh in the Arab-Zionist meeting, 29.11.21, W.A.

[74] See pp. 49-50 above.

[75] For this meeting I used two notes: a long and detailed one by the

Zionists, see note 73 above, and a brief one by E. Mills of the Colonial Office, C.O.537/855.

[76] A memo by Shuckburgh, see note 66 above; E. Mills' minutes, 30.11.21, C.O.537/855.

[77] Shuckburgh's minutes, 2.12.21, ibid.

[78] Weizmann to the Under Secretary of State, C.O., 1.12.21, C.O. 733/16 file 59977.

[79] See pp. 49-50 above.

[80] The Delegation to Churchill, 4.2.22, C.O.733/36 file 6869.

[81] Ibid, 11.2.22, ibid.

[82] See all correspondence and minutes on this affair in C.O.733/36 file 6575.

[83] Major Young's minutes to Shuckburgh, 15.2.22, and 16.2.22, C.O.733/36 file 6896; Shuckburgh's minutes to Sir J. Masterton-Smith, Under Secretary, C.O., 20.2.22, ibid.

[84] Churchill to Samuel, 21.2.22, ibid; to the Arab Delegation, 1.3.22, Cmd 1700 pp.7-8.

[85] Shuckburgh's minutes, 20.2.22, see note 83 above.

[86] Samuel's reply reached the C.O. on 25.2.22, but mysteriously came to the knowledge of the Middle East Department on 9.3.22; see Samuel to Churchill, tel. 65, 24.2.22, C.O.733/19 file 11392.

[87] Arab Delegation to Churchill, 16.3.22, C.O.733/36 file 12752; also in Cmd. 1700, p. 13.

[88] See note 86 above.

[89] Shuckburgh's minutes, 5.4.22., C.O.733/36 file 12752.

[90] Shuckburgh's minutes, 20.6.22., C.O.733/36 file 29270.

[91] Cmd. 1700 pp. 17f. (emphasis mine, M.M.).

[92] Meinertzhagen, *Middle East,* pp. 69-70; Medzini, *Esser Shanim,* p. 111.

[93] For example see Churchill to an Arab delegation in Jerusalem, 28.3.21, C.O.733/2 file 21698; in his speech in the House of Commons, 14.6.21, see note 56 above; in a memo to the Cabinet 11.8.21, CAB.24/127; Samuel in his Statement of 3rd June, see note 9 above; in conversation with Eder, see note 6 above.

[94] Weizmann to the Colonial Office, 18.6.22, C.O.733/36/292.

[95] Weizmann, *Trial,* pp. 360f.

[96] The Delegation to Churchill, 17.6.22, Cmd. 1700, pp. 24-5.

Chapter Four

THE NEW POLICY: ZIONIST AND ARAB REACTION

CO-OPERATION OR NON-CO-OPERATION: THE DILEMMA OF THE PALESTINE ZIONIST EXECUTIVE

Shortly after the Civil Administration had been set up, the Zionist Executive in London decided to transfer its central Immigration, Colonisation and Trade and Industry Departments from London to Jerusalem.[1] The transfer was apparently postponed because of the financial distress of the Zionist Organisation. However, the political crisis which followed the May Disturbances convinced the Zionists of the urgent necessity to strengthen their position in Palestine by prompt promotion of their economic and colonisation projects there.[2] Accordingly, the Twelfth Zionist Congress passed a resolution in favour of splitting the Zionist Executive between London and Jerusalem and transferring the above-mentioned departments to Jerusalem, to be headed by the Palestine members of the Executive.[3]

Although this resolution had already come into force in the autumn of 1921, the new Palestine Zionist Executive had, as we have seen, very little influence over negotiations on immigration then taking place in London. However, the renewal of immigration and the siting of the Immigration Department in Jerusalem gradually increased the participation of the Palestine Executive in the legislation and excution of immigration policy.

65

The fundamental dilemma of the Palestine Executive at that time was the conflict between maximising the growth of the Jewish National Home, despite political and economic difficulties, on the one hand, and co-operating with an Administration which pursued a policy of only gradual immigration, on the other.[4] Composed of representatives of various Jewish communities in the Diaspora which held quite different political and social views, the Executive frequently failed to come to a consensus and to produce an unequivocal solution to this dilemma. One may distinguish two dissenting and uncrystallised approaches in the Executive: one, more collaborative, realistic and relatively 'minimalist', and the second, more enthusiastic, antagonistic and relatively 'maximalist'. The lack of consolidation and the eventual balance of power between these two parties caused the Executive's policy to be generally compromising, pragmatic and sometimes even inconsistent, in order to satisfy all its members.

The 'collaborative' group of the Executive consisted of Dr. David Eder, Director of the Political Department; Dr. Arthur Ruppin, its economic expert and Director of the Colonisation Department; and Dr. Siegfried van Vriesland, its Treasurer. The 'opponents' were Menachem Ussishkin, Chairman of the Executive and Director of the Keren Kayemet (Jewish National Fund) in Palestine; Professor Hermann Pick, Director of the Immigration Department and representative of the Mizrachi — the Zionist Orthodox Movement; and Joseph Sprinzak, Director of the Labour Department and representative of Hapoel Hatzair, the moderate Labour party. The dividing line between these two viewpoints could have been due to their origins; the first group were Jews from central and western Europe while the latter came mostly from eastern Europe.

Samuel's decision, in June 1921, to allow most of the immigrants stranded in Europe because of the suspension to proceed to Palestine according to the new Regulations,[5] brought over 5,000 immigrants by the end of 1921.[6] This tide of immigration, at a time of advancing economic depression in the country, increased the unemployment rate, particularly among the newcomers.[7] Many of these immigrants did not fulfil the requirements of the new Regulations and the Administration was faced with a rather difficult dilemma: should their visas be accepted without question, or should the Regulations be strictly enforced, so that all irregular cases would be deported, regardless of their genuine visas?[8] The economic crisis, in addition to strong political agitation among the Arabs, compelled Samuel to adhere strictly to the law.[9] Nevertheless, to allow time for those already en route, Samuel agreed to accept irregular cases up until 15th January 1922. In the meantime he applied urgently to London, asking that British Consuls in Europe be instructed accordingly and that the Zionist Organisation should ensure the co-operation of its Offices in Europe with the Consuls in securing that 'no further cases of irregularity in issuing visas should occur'.[10]

Samuel's appeal to the Executive for full co-operation with the Administration in this task caused a serious division of opinion within the Palestine Executive. The question facing the Palestine Zionist Executive was whether to recognise the new policy in principle or to oppose it and avoid any collaboration in restricting immigration. Dr. Eder attacked the 'double-faced' policy of the Executive for turning a blind eye to the forgeries and irregularities carried out by the Zionist Offices and individuals, and warned that sooner or later these would be discovered and cause disputes with the Government 'which may destroy the entire work of the Executive'. He insisted on adopting Government policy and acting according to the new Regulations. Furthermore, he recommended a temporary suspension of immigration until the financial situation of the Organisation improved. Dr. Ruppin, supporting Eder's views, expressed his fear of possible strikes and demonstrations by Jewish unemployed which could cause a 'very unpleasant political situation'. Sprinzak, on the other hand, objected vigorously to any concession over stoppage of immigration and suggested bluntly 'not to interfere with the irregular work of the Palestine Offices, because the Regulations themselves obliged these Offices to work illegally. Yet, the Offices might be told to carry on their work more secretly'.[11]

Characteristically, the resolution adopted by the Executive included all divisions of opinion and suggested, indirectly, a reduction in its own control over the activities of the Palestine Offices. In effect, it asked the Palestine Offices to act according to the Regulations, making clear to them the present grave situation in Palestine, but nevertheless letting them come to their 'own conclusions' about the extent of co-operation with the British Consuls regarding control on immigration.

Samuel's insistence on acting strictly according to the Regulations, and on deporting the first irregular cases after the deadline, prevented the Executive from avoiding this question. The dilemma now before the Executive consisted of two principal questions:

a) whether to agree or to oppose in principle any deportation of Jews from Palestine, on the grounds of 'technical irregularities';

b) whether or not to participate in the final examination of these cases prior to their deportation.[12]

In the absence of Dr. Eder from Palestine, Dr. Ruppin and Harry Sacher, the legal adviser of the Executive, repeatedly urged the Executive not to 'circumvent the law' but to go along with it until such time as the present policy was revoked altogether. At the same time, they suggested asking for the presence of some Zionist observers at those examinations. Sprinzak again expressed doubts as to whether permanent co-operation of the Executive in this matter would not be interpreted as recognition of the new Regulations. In his view, a state would be reached when visas issued by British Consuls would be recognised as 'legal and final' and their holders would not be expelled. At the same time, he found a possible advantage in deportation of some immigrants, which might turn public opinion against the present policy and bring about a drastic change. Ussishkin, although sharing Sprinzak's views, did not agree about the political outcome of any deportations. In his opinion, they would first and foremost affect the prestige of the Executive itself and were liable to create a bad impression among Diaspora Jews, hampering fund-raising efforts for Palestine. Accordingly, he opposed any demonstrations, but suggested informal contacts in order to reduce deportations. This approach was eventually adopted by the Executive, which avoided a principal resolution on the question.[13]

The question of deportation soon lost its acute priority with Samuel's decision, in March 1922, to suspend all immigration temporarily 'except in very special cases'. The reasons given for that unofficial suspension were the general increase of unemployment in the country, and the Executive's unreadiness to submit the precise number of unemployed immigrants.[14] This drastic measure on the part of the Government compelled the Palestine Executive to reconsider its policy in all its aspects. As on many previous occasions, Dr. Eder again repeated his appeal for full co-operation with the Government and even recommended accepting the unofficial stoppage in order to prevent an official one, which would inevitably have increased the present tension with the Administration. But the majority of the Executive strongly objected to this, pointing out the harmful effects of such a policy.

In order to find a 'golden path' between political necessity and economic reality, the Executive conceived an original idea of creating a Labour Pool to consist of an agreed number of unemployed immigrants. The Pool, agreed and approved by the Government, was designed to regulate labour immigration more flexibly, irrespective of the oscillating demands for labour and the professional qualifications of the immigrants. It was also suggested that the Pool be maintained by the Zionist Organisation and dispersed among Jewish colonies, to avoid Arab agitation and subsequent political friction.[15]

This rather unorthodox proposal found considerable understanding and support from Morris. The Labour Pool could easily co-ordinate with Morris's fundamental conception of increasing immigration without worsening the negative effects of unemployment. Furthermore, Morris revealed to Dr. Eder his personal disagreement with the present immigration scheme and promised that Zionist responsibility for labour immigration would be increased. In practical terms, Morris tentatively agreed on a Pool of 2,500 people on condition that the Executive would remove its objection to the appointment of Immigration Officers abroad.[16]

The fact that Morris himself had various reservations about the new policy and was offering the Executive a 'deal', strengthened Eder's case for more co-operation with the Government. Eder even took upon himself to recommend these appointments to his colleagues. Pressing for more 'understanding' and 'collaboration' with the Administration, Dr. Eder stated that the Executive had to admit that 'neither it nor the Zionist Organisation's Palestine Offices had the ability to select suitable immigrants for Palestine'. Accordingly, he suggested leaving entire control over immigration in the hands of the Government. Dr. Ruppin supported Eder's views, cautiously explaining that by transferring control to these inspectors the Zionist Organisation could rid itself of such accusations as that of introducing Bolsheviks to Palestine and thus there would be no justification for any further deportation of undesirable or irregular immigrants. Nevertheless, he demanded that the primary selection of immigrants, and their adjustment to the economic needs of the country, should remain in the hands of the Zionist Palestine Offices.[17]

However, Eder and Ruppin failed to convince their colleagues. Expressing their fears that the proposed Officers would encroach on the functions of the Palestine Offices, the 'opponents' placed three conditions on their agreement: first, that the Officers must be Jewish or at least 'Christians close to our opinion'; second, that their control be limited only to examining the total fixed number and political desirability of the immigrants, leaving the actual selection to the Palestine Offices; and lastly that the Zionist Organisation should have the right to control the Officers' work. These conditions, and in particular the last one, were justified in the light of Morris's proposal that the Zionist Organisation should finance the maintenance of the proposed establishment.[18]

As will be seen in the next chapter, the question of the Immigration Officers was not in any way dependent upon Zionist consent, but rather upon more substantial factors. The severe conditions which the Executive laid down for these appointments were unrealistic and unacceptable to the Administration. Acting under enormous political pressure from both Labour circles in Palestine and the Palestine Offices in the Diaspora, the Executive was compelled to protest against any restriction on immigration; nevertheless, realising its financial distress, and its complete dependence upon the Government, it could not afford to reject the policy absolutely and avoid co-operation with the Government. Hence the pragmatic attempts to heal the breaches between the economic reality and political necessities. In these circumstances the question of co-operation with the Government was an academic if not a hypothetical one.

ARAB REJECTION OF THE CONSTITUTIONAL PROPOSALS

Following approval of the White Paper by the House of Commons, the Arab Delegation in London was ordered by the Executive of the Arab Palestine Congress to reject the White Paper officially and to return to Palestine 'at once'.[19] Opinion at the Colonial Office was that the Delegation would return to Palestine 'with failure thrown in their faces and will assuredly not allow the matter to rest there'. Colonel Richard Meinertzhagen, then Military Adviser to the Middle East Department of the Colonial Office, predicted Arab 'passive resistance' which could later on turn into 'an aggressive attitude towards Zionism and the British Administration'.[20] These fears caused the Secretary of State to send an urgent message to Samuel expressing his 'full and unhesitating support for preservation of order as [the High Commissioner] may consider necessary in event of disturbances'.[21]

However, despite urgent calls from Palestine, the Delegation preferred to prolong its stay in London. At first, they expected to have a further opportunity to meet the Secretary of State; after his refusal to see them[22] they were apparently hoping that a delay in their arrival might calm the excitement in Palestine.[23] These speculations eventually prevented the Delegation from arriving in time for the opening of the Fifth Arab Congress, due to take place late in July. The Delegation was rushed to the Congress immediately upon its arrival and the Government was thus prevented from meeting them and advising them to adopt a more moderate line in their reports to the Congress.[24]

The principal issue at the Fifth Arab Congress was the question of non-co-operation in the elections for the Legislative Council. On this matter the Congress unanimously adopted a resolution calling for a ban on the election. The argument for the resolution was derived from both ideological and practical reasons. Participation in the elections might be interpreted as 'tantamount to acceptance' of the White Paper and the Mandate. On the other hand, the limited power delegated to the proposed body far from satisfied the principal Arab demand for a representative National Government. The Congress further recommended various practical methods of propaganda to be carried out, which later proved very effective.[25]

At the same time, the Administration, having reason to believe in the existence of moderate elements among the Arab leadership and the Delegation itself, launched a comprehensive propaganda campaign in favour of vast Arab participation in the election. The main argument in this campaign was the substantial Arab opportunity of influencing future immigration policy through the proposed Immigration Committee.[26] The proposed terms of the Committee, as presented to the Arab Delegation by the Secretary of State in April 1922,[27] and later on published in the Palestine Order in Council issued in August 1922, recommended that:—

(i) The High Commissioner shall confer upon all matters relating to the regulating of immigration with a Committee consisting of not less than one half of the unofficial members of the Legislative Council, and provision shall be made by Order in Council for investing the said Committee with all such powers and authorities and otherwise for the constitution and conduct of the business of the said Committee, as may be necessary to carry this Article into effect.

(ii) In the event of any difference of opinion between the High Commissioner and the said Committee upon any such matter as aforesaid the High Commissioner shall make a full report on the subject to the Secretary of State, whose decision thereon shall be final.[28]

Despite the Arabs' outright rejection, first by the Delegation and later on by the Congress, of the Legislative Council, the Government presented the Immigration Committee as the most worthwhile consideration for the Arabs to participate in the elections. Wyndham Deedes, the Chief Secretary, who took a personal hand in conducting the official 'persuasion' campaign, was at pains to persuade Arab local and national leaders of the obvious advantages to Arab interests of the Committee. At the same time, he emphasised that taking part in the elections would not necessarily mean Arab acceptance of the Balfour Declaration.[29]

Meanwhile, the Administration was preparing for the elections. As a preliminary stage the Government intended to hold a population census in October 1922. This decision placed the Arab Executive in a rather difficult dilemma. Although results of the census would have shown an overwhelming Arab majority, their participation might be interpreted as a departure from their decision to boycott the elections. After lengthy deliberations the Arab Executive issued a notice informing the public that the census was of 'public benefit'.[30] Nevertheless, the Government, having some reason to believe that there might be opposition to the census, issued a warning that refusal to register or cause others to refuse to register was illegal and punishable. It seems that this warning, and a further Government decision to prosecute individuals and the Arab Executive as a body, should they continue their agitation, induced the Executive to co-operate with the Administration.[31]

However, the Government's success in carrying the census into effect could not ensure a similar result regarding the elections. The essential difference between the two was obvious. The census was compulsory, while participation in the elections was left to personal decision. Moreover, the avoidance of compulsory measures to force participation was interpreted by the Arabs as official consent to the boycott.[32] In any case, the Government's liberal policy was hardly able to compete with the vigorous campaign conducted by the Arab Executive. Under these circumstances, the elections were bound to fail.[33] Only 18 per cent of the Moslems and 5.5 per cent of the Christian Arabs, as compared with 50 per cent of the Jewish voters, used their right to vote.[34]

These anticipated, but nevertheless very remarkable, results did not convince the High Commissioner that Arab non-co-operation was absolute and genuine. Samuel tended to believe that political apathy in general, lack of confidence in the candidates and a feeling that the "Legislative Council would not bring any better protection to the Arab interests" played a decisive role in their political behaviour.[35] This conclusion persuaded him to recommend the reconstitution of an Advisory Council consisting of nominated representatives, identical with the composition of the Legislative Council, namely, eight Moslems, two Jews and two Christian members.[36] Accordingly, Samuel suggested an amendment of the Palestine Order in Council 1922, which would consider the new body.[37]

The idea of consulting the population on questions regarding immigration was not abandoned in this proposal. On the contrary, the High Commissioner considered the entire constitution of the proposed Council to be the fulfilment of his policy in favour of consulting the people of Palestine 'on a matter so closely affecting their interests'.[38] Nevertheless, the proposed powers of the new Council in regard to immigration policy were not defined in the new Order, nor in the High Commissioner's Statement of 29th May, in which he presented the proposed Council. These were left open for further negotiations with Arab and Zionist leaders then in progress, under the leadership of Gilbert Clayton, the newly appointed Chief Secretary.[39]

With these negotiations still taking place in Palestine a new Arab Delegation, which had been elected at the June 1923 Sixth Arab Congress, left for London. Immediately after its arrival, the Delegation demanded an opportunity to lay the Arab cause before a special Cabinet Committee which was then discussing future British policy in Palestine.[40]

The principal recommendation of the Committee was the immediate constitution of an Arab Agency in Palestine which would occupy a position 'exactly analogous to that accorded to the Jewish Agency under the terms of the Mandate'. It was suggested that the Arab Agency should be a recognised body for the purpose of advice and co-operation with the Administration in such matters 'as may affect the interests of the non-Jewish population'. As far as control over immigration was concerned it would have the right to be consulted as to the means of ensuring that the 'rights and position' of the non-Jewish sections of the population were not prejudiced by Jewish immigration. In practical terms it was proposed that the Arab Agency, in conjunction with the Jewish Agency, would take the place of the Immigration Committee for the function indicated in Article 84 of the Palestine Order in Council.[41] However, this arrangement was considered by the Secretary of State to be a provisional settlement only, subject to review whenever a fully representative Legislative Council was set up.[42]

The Arab Delegation was neither invited to put its case before the Committee,[43] nor informed of its recommendations.[44] The opinion of the Palestine Government and Colonial Office was that consultations with the Delegation at that stage would inevitably have hampered the Chief Secretary's effort to set up the Advisory Council.[45] Nevertheless, the damage had been done. Reports reaching Palestine that the Delegation's activities in London were producing 'good results' and that 'success is imminent' caused the Arab candidates to refrain from taking their seats in the Council. They apparently feared that if they were to do so, they would have been 'solely responsible' for any failure of the Delegation. In these circumstances, Clayton was unable to fill the vacancies on the Council and its constitution was postponed.[46]

The formation of an Arab Agency had no better chances. Three months after its approval by the Cabinet, the Report of the Cabinet Committee was presented to Arab representatives by the High Commissioner and was unanimously rejected. Musa Kazim Pasha, President of the Arab Delegation, stated on behalf of those present that the Arabs, 'having never recognised the status of the Jewish Agency, have no desire for the establishment of an Arab Agency on the same basis'.[47]

With that statement, the proposal to set up an Arab Agency, together with the entire idea of closer association of the Arab community with the Administration in matters which might affect their interests, was brought to an end. The failure of the three successive British attempts to establish a Legislative Council, to reconstruct the Advisory Council and to set up an Arab Agency brought the Secretary of State to the inevitable conclusion that further efforts on similar lines would be 'useless' and that there was no other alternative than 'to continue to administer the country in conformity with their undertakings even though they have to forgo the assistance that they had hoped to obtain from the Arab community'.[48]

There is no doubt that if the Arabs had accepted the British proposals and co-operated in setting up the proposed constitutional institutions, they would have succeeded to a certain extent in influencing immigration policy. However, the extent of such influence and how matters would have been had they given their co-operation remain hypothetical questions to which only speculative answers can be given.[49] It may therefore be preferable to examine the real influence of their non-co-operation.

First, one should note the fact that, parallel to the Government's attempts to set up the proposed institutions, two separate activities were taking place, both of which had a stronger connection with immigration policy: the re-organisation of the Immigration Department, and the legislative and diplomatic activities surrounding the immigration scheme and Immigration Ordinance, both of which we shall deal with in the next chapters.

Activity surrounding the formation of the Legislative Council was conducted between August 1922, with the publication of the Palestine Order in Council, and March 1923, when the final results of the elections for the Council were received. During this period, the intention to expand the functions of the Immigration Department, or at least preserve its present state, was dominant. This aim had two main causes, administrative and political. Samuel was aware that the establishment of an Immigration Committee would give the Department a great deal of work in preparing rules to govern the Committee and its activities, necessitating the continued existence of the Department.[50] Second, the proposed formation of the Committee, which the Zionists regarded with 'gravest disfavour',[51] was likely to be accompanied by a second blow to the Zionist cause, namely the abolition of the Department. A strong Immigration Department, which the Zionists considered of 'national value' and a 'symbol', could provide some counterbalance to the Immigration Committee.[52] In this manner, the proposal to constitute the Immigration Committee gave reason for the continued existence of the Department, at least as far as Samuel was concerned.

This proposal had a very similar impact on negotiations over the new Immigration Scheme taking place in Palestine and London at that time. The readiness of the Colonial Office to meet Zionist demands with regard to the new scheme of control was strengthened in the light of the impending formation of the Immigration Committee. On this issue, the Colonial Office accepted the Zionist view 'that the argumentative position of the Palestine Government vis-a-vis the Immigration Committee will be considerably strengthened if the Committee, when it meets, finds a well considered scheme already in operation'.[53] Therefore it is not merely coincidental that, in the very week of the elections in Palestine, the Colonial Office despatched to Jerusalem the final draft of the Immigration Scheme, which went 'far to satisfy' the Zionist Organisation.[54]

However, the failure of the elections brought about a turning point in the British attitude towards Zionist demands. Samuel insisted that the reconstructed Advisory Council, as a 'representative body of the population of Palestine', should be consulted on questions regarding immigration.[55] Later on, he removed his previous objection to abolishing the Department of Immigration and Travel, also suggesting that Morris, who was favoured by the Zionists, be dismissed and that Hyamson be appointed Chief Controller.[56] Moreover, in July 1923, the Colonial Office was considering a new scheme for limiting the entire Jewish immigration.[57] This new course and the appointment of the Cabinet Committee to consider future policy in Palestine brought tension with the Zionists to an unprecedented head. Weizmann called at the Colonial Office at the end of July and in an extraordinarily stormy appearance criticised the appointment of the Cabinet Committee, the 'concessions' to the Arab Delegation and the intention to limit immigration numerically.[58]

The rejection of the proposal to set up an Arab Agency by Arab representatives in November 1923 only contributed to the independence of the Government from both Zionist and Arab appeals. The outcome of this policy was expressed accordingly in the new Immigration Ordinance and Regulations which will be dealt with in the next chapter. All in all, it seems quite obvious that Arab policy had a negative impact on Zionist demands and immigration policy as a whole. If it had been expected that Arab non-co-operation would improve British-Zionist relations, reality showed the exact opposite. According to the British policy of 'equilibrium' in Palestine, this outcome was inevitable.

Thus far we have seen the impact of Arab policy on various questions regarding Jewish immigration. The influence of these matters over the Arab stand, however, was negligible. Nevertheless, the actual volume of immigration during the period concerned did have a considerable effect on the Arab stand regarding British constitutional proposals. One may assume that had negotiations over these proposals taken place during 1924-1925, when Jewish immigration reached an unexpected peak, their outcome might have been different. There is no doubt that the economic distress of the Zionist Organisation, the high rate of unemployment, the ebb in immigration and comparative increase in emigration from Palestine during those years, all contributed to a hardening of the Arab stand. Under these circumstances it might have seemed to the Arabs that there was very little to lose by not co-operating with the Administration. This assumption is strengthened in the light of the Arabs' readiness during 1924-1926 to renew negotiations for setting up representative institutions and an Immigration Committee, in which Jewish representation would be even stronger than in the original British proposal, i.e. five members of whom two would be Jews, two Arabs and a British official as Chairman.[59]

NOTES

[1] See resolution of the Z.E., 10.8.20., C.Z.A., Z4/302/3A.

[2] 'The Jaffa Events' — 'circular letter to members of the Action Committee and Presidents of Zionist Federations', 1.7.20., W.A.; also Leonard Stein's report 'The Situation in Palestine, August 1921', 17.9.21., C.O.733/16 file 52260.

[3] Zionist Organisation, *'report of the Twelfth Zionist Congress',* London 1922.

[4] See minutes of P.Z.E. meeting, 15.12.21., C.Z.A. unclassified.

[5] The announcement of the new policy was made in the H.C.'s statement of 3rd June, see above, pp. 37-8. The new Regulations of August 1921 were issued in the Official Gazette No. 49, of August 15th 1921, see App. 3.

[6] 5039 immigrants; see App. 6.

[7] Samuel to Churchill, 14.12.21., tel. 502, C.O.733/8 file 62256.

[8] Ibid, ibid.

[9] 'Political Situation in Palestine', Samuel to Churchill, 9.3.22., confidential despatch, C.O.733/19 file 13502.

[10] Samuel to Churchill, 14.12.21., see note 7 above.

[11] See note 4 above.

[12] Minutes of P.Z.E. meeting, 19.2.22., C.Z.A.

[13] Ibid, ibid.

[14] Eder in P.Z.E. meeting, 28.3.22., C.Z.A.

[15] Pick, ibid.

[16] Eder in P.Z.E. meeting, 10.4.22., also in 11.4.22.

[17] See the general debate on this question in P.Z.E. minutes of meetings on 10.4.22.; 11.4.22.; 10.5.22.; C.Z.A.

[18] Eder in P.Z.E. meeting of 10.5.22., C.Z.A.

[19] See telegrams from Omar Bitar, President, Executive, Palestine Arab Congress to the Sec. of State for the Colonies, 8.7.22.; also petitions from Moslem-Christian and Nadi Arabi Associations and from 'representatives of all Palestine districts' of the same date, all in C.O.733/36 file 33005. Also Musa Kazim el Husseini, President of the Arab Delegation, to Churchill, 10.7.22., C.O.733/36 file 33276.

[20] See memorandum of R. Meinertzhagen, C.O., 6.7.22., and minutes of Major Young, 8.7.22., 12.7.22., ibid.

[21] Churchill to Samuel, tel. 213, 14.7.22., ibid.

[22] See Young's minutes, note 20 above.

[23] Wyndham Deedes, Chief Secretary, Palestine, to J. Shuckburgh, C.O., 'personal and confidential', 15.9.22, C.O.733/38 file 48206.

[24] Ibid, ibid.

[25] On the Congress's debates, resolutions and recommendations, see Porath, *Emergence,* pp. 110-11, 148-9.

[26] On the Government's campaign see file 2/242/1.

[27] Churchill to the Pal. Arab Delegation, 11.4.22., Cmd. 1700, 1922.

[28] Article 84 of the Order, Cmd. 1889, 1923.

[29] See Porath, *Emergence,* pp. 151-2.

[30] See 'Appeal to the Noble Nation' by the Executive Committee of the Fifth Palestinian-Arab Congress, 15.10.22, enclosed in H.C.'s 'Report on the Political Situation . . .', October 1922, 'secret' C.O.733/27 file 57552.

[31] Deedes to Shuckburgh, 20.10.22, C.O.733/38 file 53952; also Public Notice issued by the Pal. Govt. (undated) and 'Proclamation to the Noble Nation' by the Arab Executive (undated), both in the H.C.'s report, ibid.

[32] Porath, *Emergence,* p. 152-3.

[33] See Samuel's 'anticipations' a month before the election took place, in his despatch to the Duke of Devonshire, Churchill's successor at the C.O., tel. 32, 27.1.23, C.O.733/41 file 5099.

[34] Samuel to Devonshire, tel. 76, 10.3.23, C.O.733/43 file 12857; also tel. 123, 11.4.23, in paper 18303, ibid; and his official Report, 11.5.23, in Cmd. 1889, 1923.

[35] Samuel's Report, 11.5.23, ibid.

[36] See 'text of announcement' published by the High Commissioner on 29th May, brought in his despatch to the Secretary of State, 1.6.23, Cmd. 1889.

[37] See 'The Palestine (Amendment) Order in Council, 1923', ibid.

[38] Samuel to Devonshire, confidential despatch, 20.4.23, I.S.A. 11/1/1/I.

[39] G. Clayton, Acting H.C. to Sec. of State, tel. 276, C.O.733/48 file 38851.

[40] The Palestine Arab Delegation to the Chairman, Cabinet Committee (Pal), 22.8.23, C.O.733/58 file 37403.

[41] See Pal. Committee, *The Future of Palestine,* Report, 27.7.23, Cab 23/46; Devonshire to Clayton, tel. 247, 3.8.23, C.O.733/48 file 38851.

[42] The Secretary of State to the H.C., 4.10.23, C.O.733/58 file 42044, published as well in Cmd. 1989, 1923.

[43] This was decided even before its arrival in London. Shuckburgh noted: 'I understand that it would be quite contrary to general practice that the Cabinet Committee should invite witnesses and hear evidence', and added, 'if the Committee hears the Delegation the Zionists will unquestionably demand to be heard as well . . .' Minutes on 16.7.23, C.O.733/54 file 35998; see also his minutes on 24.7.23, C.O.733/54 file 37431.

[44] Devonshire to Clayton 'personal and secret' tel. 247, 3.8.23, C.O.733/48 file 38851.

[45] Samuel to Devonshire, tel. 317, 21.9.23, I.S.A., 2/171; Devonshire to Samuel, tel. 287, 22.9.23, ibid.

[46] Acting H.C. to Sec. of State, tel. 276, 3.8.23, C.O.733/48 file 38851.

[47] H.C. to Sec. of State, 11.10.23; see also detailed report enclosed in H.C.'s despatch 1041, 12.10.23, C.O.733/50 file 51395, both published in Cmd. 1989, 1923.

[48] Sec. of State to H.C., tel. 331, 9.11.23, C.O.733/50 file 51553, published also in Cmd. 1989.

[49] See for example Porath, *Emergence,* pp. 156-8.

[50] H.C. to Sec. of State, Despatch 245, 18.4.22, C.O.733/21 file 20456.

[51] See notes by Leonard Stein on interview with Major Young, 'confidential', 27.2.23, C.Z.A. S6/275.

[52] Dr. Weizmann at meeting with H.C. and Palestine senior officials, 5.12.22, I.S.A.11/6.

[53] Stein to Kisch, 'personal', 16.1.23, C.Z.A. Z4/16085.

[54] Kisch to Secretary, Zionist Organisation, London, 11.3.23, C.Z.A. Z4/16085.

[55] Samuel to Devonshire 'confidential', 20.4.23, I.S.A. 11/1/1I.

[56] See Chapter 5, pp. 91-2.

[57] Shuckburgh's memorandum, 24.7.23, C.O.733/54 file 37431.

[58] Compare Weizmann and Shuckburgh's versions of the same meeting: Weizmann's in C.Z.A. Z4/16060, 'secret'; Shuckburgh's in note to the Secretary of State, 26.7.23, C.O.733/54 file 37431. See also Weizmann to Duke of Devonshire (following that meeting) 26.7.23, C.Z.A. Z4/16060.

[59] Kisch to Stein, 7.11.24, C.Z.A. Z4/1445 IX.

Chapter Five

REORGANISATION OF THE DEPARTMENT OF IMMIGRATION AND TRAVEL: ATTEMPTS TO ADJUST ITS MACHINERY TO THE NEW SCHEME OF CONTROL

THE TENDENCY TOWARDS EXTENSION

The revision of immigration policy caused Samuel to extend the functions of the Immigration Department and to adjust it to the new scheme of control. As early as November 1921, he set up a new Sub-Department of Labour as a section of the Department of Immigration and Travel. Its duties were to collect information on the labour market and to estimate the future demands of manpower in the various economic spheres. This estimate could help regulate immigration according to the categories of immigrants upon which the new scheme was based.[1] However, the Sub-Department's task was not restricted to Jewish immigrants only, but included the whole population of Palestine. Samuel saw this as a vital correction of injustice to Arab labour, whose employment problems had so far received no consideration from the Government.[2]

Albert M. Hyamson, a former official of the Central Zionist Office in London and, from January 1921, the Assistant Director of the Department of Immigration and Travel, was appointed Controller of Labour. Samuel believed that the fact that Hyamson was a Jew and a past active Zionist would not prevent him from conducting this delicate job fairly and genuinely.[3] In this way, another problem, the increasing personal rivalry in the Department between Hyamson and Morris, had been partly solved. Hyamson, who had acted as Director of the Department during Morris's mission to Europe in the summer of 1921, had apparently taken advantage of his superior's absence and persuaded the Chief Secretary to split up the Immigration Department, himself becoming head of the new Sub-Department.[4]

A larger and more complicated extension of the Department's function was anticipated with the proposed appointment of Immigration Officers in the main centres of immigration in Europe. Samuel's first objection to this proposal, originally recommended by Morris,[5] was due to his assumption that the new policy would inevitably reduce immigration and would not justify the existence of this expensive network in Europe.[6] Nevertheless, the inefficient control exposed by British Consuls,[7] and the Colonial Office's support of Morris's proposals,[8] caused the Palestine Administration to drop its previous objection and agree to the appointment of three Inspectors and not only one as the Colonial Office had recommended.[9] Samuel placed two necessary conditions upon these appointments: first, that the Inspectors should be accorded the status of Vice Consul, and second, that their expenses be met by revenues accruing from fees for visas, endorsements and the like.[10]

The Foreign Office's first reaction to these appointments was rather disappointing. Lord Curzon, the Foreign Secretary, felt that the execution of the scheme 'would not only create an undesirable precedent to break the universal procedure and to establish new rules for Palestine only, but that it might also give rise in practice to difficult questions with Foreign Governments'. Nevertheless, he consented to the appointments, on condition that the Inspectors should not have the power to issue visas and take fees themselves, but only to recommend applicants to the British Consul for a visa.[11]

The rejection of Samuel's conditions by the Foreign Office, which could have called the whole new immigration scheme into question, compelled Jerusalem to spur the Colonial Office on towards reaching a more satisfactory arrangement.[12] Writing to London, the Palestine Government re-emphasised the inefficiency of the British Consuls in controlling immigration, which had been the indirect cause of unemployment in the country, and insisted on the early appointment of Immigration Officers in order to 'secure adequate control over Consuls and Zionist representatives abroad'. Furthermore, the proposed Inspectors were considered 'essential to the satisfactory conduct of the new immigration scheme for selecting immigrants most suited to the economic needs of the country'.[13] The Colonial Office, although for different reasons, did not need much encouragement on this issue. In its opinion, Immigration Officers abroad would definitely be vital in preventing any infiltration of 'undesirable elements' and in supervising the work of the Zionist Offices in order to put a stop to unfair discrimination against non-Zionist applicants.[14]

The different reasons given to justify these appointments might illustrate the different approaches of London and Jerusalem to the Zionist role in the new scheme. While Samuel still insisted on granting sole authority of control to the Immigration Officers (by relieving the Palestine Zionist Offices of their previous privileges), the Colonial Office (according to its agreement with the Zionists at the Immigration Conference of November 1921)[15] was inclined to support the restoration of the old Certificate system, by recommending that the Palestine Offices exercise considerable discretion over selection and regulation of immigrants.[16]

However, without a solution to the problem of financing the proposed establishment, the scheme could not go far. Opinion at the Foreign Office was that the Palestine Immigration Officers should be allowed to collect additional fees as well as His Majesty's Consuls and thus enable the Palestine Government to make up some of the £5,000 required for the scheme.[17] Morris, on the other hand, suggested that the Zionist Organisation itself should bear the expenses of the Officers who were intended to control its own work.[18] This proposal, although not entirely rejected by the Zionists,[19] had a very slim chance of being accepted by the Palestine Government because of its contradictory nature.

The solution to this financial deadlock eventually came from a quite unexpected direction. The increasing disagreement between Egypt and Palestine regarding the traffic of Jewish immigrants through Egypt compelled the Foreign Office to intervene and to request consultations with the Colonial Office.[20] This development gave the Colonial Office a fresh opportunity to bring up the question of Immigration Officers before the Foreign Office. At an inter-Departmental Conference at the Foreign Office on April 5th 1922, the entire question of control over immigration was considered. The Colonial Office based its arguments on recent reports from Palestine accusing the Consuls of oversights in control over immigration. They succeeded in persuading the Foreign Office to remove its objection to Samuel's condition that the proposed Officers should be self-supporting, their revenues being fees paid for visas, endorsements etc. The Foreign Office then applied to the Treasury, requesting that the Government 'should make no claim for any fees paid by the prospective immigrants', using the argument that the establishment of such officers 'would be of considerable assistance to His Majesty's Consuls and would no doubt relieve them of a large part of their work'.[21]

Following the Treasury's approval,[22] Foreign Office officials found 'the way now clear' to installing the proposed Officers at Warsaw, Vienna and particularly at Trieste, where they were interested in maintaining 'a proper organisation, in view of the immigrant traffic in transit to Egypt'.[23] Nevertheless, the Colonial Office, which had at the same time issued its 'Declaration of British Policy in Palestine' (Cmd. 1700), held the view 'that it would be unwise for any new procedure to be adopted until such time as the Legislative Council has come into being and the Immigration Committee [of this body] had been consulted upon the whole question'.[24] However Samuel, anxious to see the early establishment of the scheme, emphasised that the appointment of the Immigration Officers 'does not imply any radical change' in the present method of control and would co-ordinate with the future policy. Furthermore, in his view, it would be regarded locally 'as indicative of fulfilment' of the undertaking given in his own Statement of 3rd June 1921, 'that the Immigration Department would be entirely responsible for the supervision of immigration'.[25] The High Commissioner then submitted a detailed estimate of the cost of the proposed establishment of three inspectors which now amounted to £6,661 per annum, while revenues expected from visa fees of 10,000 immigrants and 2,000 regular travellers at £1 each, amounted to £12,000.[26]

Following the approval of the White Paper by Parliament, the Colonial Office initiated a second inter-Departmental Conference with the Foreign Office, to discuss the immigration question in all its aspects. Among other decisions, the Conference passed a resolution on the immediate appointment of four Immigration Officers at Warsaw, Vienna, Constantinople and Trieste, 'in order that they familiarise themselves with the present condition of immigration during the period required for the completion of the machinery for putting the new scheme into force'.[27]

Despite this resolution, Foreign Office officials expressed serious doubts regarding Samuel's estimate of the cost of the new machinery, since the regular visa fee was eight shillings and not £1 and since travellers were to pay their fees to the British Consuls and not to the Immigration Officer. The Foreign Office came to the inevitable conclusion that Samuel's proposals were over-optimistic and contrary to Treasury instructions, and that the estimated revenue of the Immigration Department was unlikely to be realised, unless immigration were to increase considerably.[28]

THE TENDENCY TOWARDS REDUCTION

The principle that immigrants and visitors to Palestine should maintain the entire establishment of the Department of Immigration and Travel by paying various fees (for visa, landing, immigration, etc.) was a fundamental one and had existed since the very formation of the Department.[29] This principle, although of an economic nature, also had important political significance, as it could be shown to the public that Jewish immigration was not a burden on the Palestinian taxpayer.

Following the May Disturbances and increasing criticism in Great Britain and Palestine of the Government's so-called 'pro-Zionist' policy, the Palestine Administration had to send a notice to the press, pointing out that 'none of the cost of the Department of Immigration and Travel is being paid by the taxpayers of Palestine' and that the Department showed a surplus which had been carried over to the credit of the General Revenue.[30] Nevertheless, it seemed very likely that Samuel's intention to extend the functions of the Department in order to restrict control on immigration could have increased its expenses. However, this restriction and the decision to abolish fees for passports as from January 1922 could only reduce the Department's revenue and turn its profit into a heavy deficit.[31] At the same time, pressure from the Secretariat to reduce the Department's staff met with strong objections from Morris.[32]

These contradictory approaches within the Palestine Administration brought about the intervention of the Colonial Office, which recommended nothing less than the complete abolition of the Department by delegating its existing functions to other Departments in the following order: the issuing of passports and the entire control of immigration policy to the Secretariat; actual control of entry into the country to the Director General of Police and Prisons; and the Sub-Department of Labour as a whole to the Department of Industry and Commerce.[33]

Samuel was totally opposed to these proposals, mainly for administrative reasons. The recent restrictions on immigration, explained the High Commissioner, 'give rise to a great deal of controversy' and 'provide extremely difficult problems to be solved', which required much attention, more than the Secretariat could devote to them. Moreover, the establishment of the proposed Board of Immigration and the legislative work on immigration would necessitate the continued existence of the Department. The High Commissioner went on to explain that if this work were to be undertaken by the Secretariat, it would require practically the same staff as was at present employed by the Department and no economy would be achieved. But to avoid a hasty decision, he suggested postponing the whole matter until he had discussed it with the Colonial Office during his impending visit to London.[34]

As the general question of re-organising the entire Palestine Administration was discussed at Samuel's meetings at the Colonial Office, it was decided to leave the fate of the Immigration Department, among other issues, in the hands of an Economy Committee to be set up in Jerusalem.[35] The Committee, consisting of three members including Hyamson and an official of the Secretariat, gave considerable support to the Colonial Office proposals, in opposition to the stands taken by Samuel and Morris. Among its constructive proposals the Committee recommended, first, to transfer part of the present duties of the Department, such as travel facilities, admission of immigrants and registration of British subjects to the Director General of Police and Prisons and second, to adopt the Secretariat's proposal of reducing the Department's staff by closing the Jaffa Immigration Office, scaling down the Haifa Office and having the Jerusalem Office exclusively for granting visas. In addition to this, it was suggested that the appointment of the Immigration Officers abroad be postponed, since the anticipated revenue from visa fees would not have justified their existence. If the above recommendations were carried into effect, the Committee promised a considerable saving of £6,175, one third of the Department's total budget.[36]

As expected, the Committee's proposals brought immediate criticism from the Immigration Department. Morris attacked the Committee's basic estimate of revenue for the coming year which was based on the present low rate of immigration. He foresaw that this would soon change for the better as a result of the recent approval of the Mandate, the approaching economic prosperity and the most probable increase of immigration from Russia, which would follow the stationing of British Consuls in Moscow and Odessa. The expected increase in immigration would accordingly augment the Department's revenue from immigration fees. Referring to the proposed transfer of certain functions to the Police, Morris objected to this on political grounds, stating that 'from the point of view of the tender susceptibilities of the

Palestine public, there are grave objections to the Police and Prison stations being used for this purpose'.[37]

As Director of the Department, Morris was naturally interested in raising its standard and extending its functions. The realisation of these aims depended mainly on the financial state of the Department, and there were two possible ways of increasing its revenue; one, by raising fees for various services and the other by increasing the number of immigrants and travellers. The first possibility met with strong and persistent objections from the Zionist Organisation as well as from foreign Governments such as France and Italy, which considered themselves defenders of the interests of Christian pilgrims to the Holy Land.[38] The second possibility was even more complicated, as it contradicted the entire spirit of the new immigration policy. Morris, who personally admired the 'creative, energetic and initiative' nature of the Jewish people and believed that Jewish immigration was a 'promising element', which might prosper and enrich Palestine,[39] inclined to the second choice, namely that of facilitating Jewish immigration. Having personal objections to the new policy, Morris was undoubtedly not the ideal person to execute it efficiently. His constant disagreements with this policy eventually led to his dismissal one year later. However, at this stage, Samuel preferred not to interfere and sent the Committee's reports with Morris's observations, without submitting any personal comments. This non-committal attitude was not entirely welcomed by the Colonial Office, which expected the High Commissioner to add his own views on the issue and, if possible, to recommend concrete proposals for reducing the Department.[40]

Following the failure of the Palestine Legislative Council elections in February 1923, which prevented the constitution of the Immigration Committee, Samuel was obliged to return to this unpleasant question, but now deprived of his previous argument, which was based on the necessity of the Department as an 'auxiliary body' to the Immigration Committee. He was then compelled to reveal the real reason for his objection, namely the firm Zionist pressure against any weakening of the Immigration Department, which they considered 'as the material expression or symbol of the upbuilding of the Jewish National Home'.[41] Writing to London, Samuel expressed serious doubts as to whether the recommendations of the Committee would really lead to any economies and emphasised the political undesirability of any association of the Police with immigration.[42]

Although Colonial Office reservations about the Committee's findings stemmed mainly from economic and administrative reasons,[43] the Duke of Devonshire, Churchill's successor at the Colonial Office, was ready to accept Samuel's point of view. Nevertheless, the Secretary of State insisted that those parts of the Committee's proposals which did not conflict with Samuel's anxiety about Zionist criticism should be carried out, in order to effect some saving in the Department. Accordingly, he recommended that all functions concerned with travel be transferred to the Department of Public Security, and other trivial duties not directly concerned with immigration to the Secretariat and the Police. The new re-organised Department would then deal exclusively with matters regarding immigration, which might permit a substantial reduction in its budget.[44]

Samuel rejected these proposals again, this time for economic as well as political reasons. Firstly, he was opposed to maintaining two separate authorities, each dealing with certain classes of incomers to Palestine, which in his opinion would inevitably lead 'to confusion and more expenses'. Secondly, the proposed formation of the Department exclusively for immigrants might harm its 'common image' and emphasise its 'completely Jewish aspect', which was undesirable from all points of view. Samuel instead suggested an amalgamation of the Sub-Department of Labour with Immigration and Travel, placing control of the combined Department directly in the hands of the Secretariat. It might thus be possible to settle all the controversial questions concerned with the Department. The combined Department would become a section of the Secretariat and the question of its profitability would then lose its political significance; second, a probable saving of £2,000 (the sum required by the Colonial Office) could then be effected and direct control over the policy and machinery of immigration would be strengthened.[45]

Supervision of the Section would be further improved by Samuel's further suggestion that Morris be dismissed from his post and Hyamson appointed as Chief of the proposed Permits Section. Hyamson, who had proved himself so far to be a very energetic, meticulous and obedient official, and more important, able to keep the Zionists in strict check, was certainly a more suitable person to implement the restrictions on immigration.[46] The official reason given for this reshuffle was that additional efforts were to be made in reducing the Department's expenses. Since Morris appeared in the list of staff as a temporary officer, whereas Hyamson was listed as permanent, it was considered 'clearly fair' that Morris should go and Hyamson remain.[47]

At the same time, Samuel did not try to conceal his own fears about probable opposition to his proposals, from both Arab as well as Jewish circles. The Zionists, stated the High Commissioner, might regard the abolition of the Department with 'apprehensive dismay', while the Arabs could consider the appointment of a Jew as Chief of the Section as further evidence 'that control over immigration is entirely in Jewish hands'.[48]

Samuel's visit to London in summer 1923 provided a suitable opportunity for wide-ranging discussion on the future of the Immigration Department and the fate of Hyamson and Morris. Colonial Office officials were firm in their opinion that any attempt to place a Jew in charge of immigration was bound to be interpreted 'as a mere manoeuvre to get rid of a Christian in favour of a Jew and to place the Department under Zionist domination'. It was therefore agreed to adopt Samuel's proposals concerning the reorganisation of the Department and removal of Morris from his post, but to transfer Hyamson to a different position and place the new Section under an officer who was neither Arab nor Jew.[49] Ironically, it was the Zionists and not the Arabs who regarded unfavourably the idea of removing Morris and placing Hyamson in charge of immigration.[50]

Nevertheless, when the Permit Section eventually came into being on 1st April 1924, Hyamson was the man to be appointed as its chief.[51] However, this event was followed by an unusual incident. Shortly after his appointment, Hyamson addressed a memorandum to the Chief Secretary in which he outlined the functions of the new Section and pointed out that most of them 'are directly concerned with labour', while the 'least important are not even remotely connected with immigration'. Moreover, he considered immigration itself to be 'mainly a labour matter' and insisted on changing the section's title from 'Permits' to 'Labour'.[52] Although neither Samuel[53] nor the Colonial Office[54] considered Hyamson's proposals too seriously, his arguments do shed some light upon his personal concept of immigration, and his new task in particular.

The original motive for re-organising the Department of Immigration and Travel was to extend its functions, in order to adjust its machinery to the new scheme of control. But the economic depression, the grave unemployment and consequently the ebb of immigration affected its revenue and eventually caused its reduction and abolition as an independent unit. However, its new status was in line with present policy and was designed to act more efficiently and strictly. Ironically, after the new machinery had just been set up and Hyamson had taken over, Morris's predictions of approaching economic prosperity, followed by a tide of immigration,[55] began to come true. The new machinery of control had now to face an entirely different reality from that for which it had originally been intended.

NOTES

[1] See 'Meeting held in the presence of His Excellency the High Commissioner to discuss the foundation of a Labour Department', 16.11.21, I.S.A. 2/145; also a note of E. Keith-Roach, First Assistant, Chief Secretary, to the H.C., 28.11.21, I.S.A. 2/218; Samuel to Churchill in a report on Civil Service, 5.12.21, despatch 496, C.O.733/8 file 63945.
[2] Samuel to Churchill, 26.12.21, Despatch 546, C.O.733/8 file 1341.
[3] Samuel to Churchill, 5.12.21, see note 1 above.

[4] E. Keith-Roach, then official in the Middle East Dept., C.O., minutes, 21.6.24, C.O.733/68 file 26356.

[5] See Morris's proposals in 'Memo. on Immigration into Palestine', 30.5.21, I.S.A. 11/3.

[6] Samuel to Churchill, 4.10.21, tel. 405, C.O.733/6 file 49714; see Chapter 3, pp. 39-40.

[7] Samuel to Churchill, 14.12.21, tel. 502, C.O.733/8, file 62256; Wyndham Deedes, Acting H.C. to Churchill, 10.3.21, confidential despatch, C.O.733/19 file 13505.

[8] G.L.M. Clauson, Middle East Department, C.O., minutes, 7.10.21, C.O.733/6 file 44737.

[9] Wyndham Deedes to Churchill, 30.12.21, tel. 521, C.O.733/8 file 245.

[10] Samuel to Churchill, 20.1.22, Despatch 23, C.O.733/18 file 4591.

[11] F.O. to C.O., 23.1.22, 'Immediate', F.O. 372/1916 file T188/147/388; C.O. to H.C., 27.1.22, tel. 29, ibid.

[12] H.C. to C.O., 11.2.22, tel. 50, ibid.

[13] Wyndham Deedes to Churchill, 11.5.22, confidential despatch, C.O.733/21, file 24592.

[14] John Shuckburgh, minutes, 2.2.22, C.O.733/18 file 4741.

[15] See Chapter 3 above, pp. 49-50.

[16] See Chapter 6 below, pp. 96-7.

[17] Eric G. Forbes-Adam, Treaty Department, F.O., minutes 23.2.22, F.O. 372/1916 file T2127/147/388.

[18] Dr. David M. Eder, Director of Political Department, P.Z.E., minutes of 56th Meeting of the Executive, 10.4.22, C.Z.A., unclassified.

[19] See Chapter 4 above, pp. 69-70.

[20] Forbes-Adam, minutes, 25.2.22, see note 17 above. For the entire question of transit through Egypt, see F.O. 372/1916 file T2389/147/388.

[21] F.O. to the Treasury, 8.5.22, F.O. 372/1916 file T5156/147/388.

[22] Treasury to F.O., 17.6.22, F.O. 372/1917 file T7217/147/388.

[23] Forbes-Adam, Minutes, 20.6.22, ibid; see also his minutes of 24.8.22, F.O. 372/1918 file T9892/147/388.

[24] Churchill to Samuel, 6.7.22, confidential despatch, C.O.733/36 file 29635.

[25] Samuel to Churchill, 22.7.22, confidential despatch, C.O.733/23 file 37766.

[26] Enclosed in Samuel's confidential despatch, 22.7.22, ibid.

[27] See minutes of the inter-Departmental Conference held at the C.O., 14.8.22, F.O.372/1918 file T9643/147/388.

[28] Forbes-Adam, minutes, 24.8.22, F.O.372/1918 file T9892/147/388; F.O. to C.O., 6.9.22, ibid.

[29] See Chapter 1 above, notes 26 and 27.

[30] 'Cost of Control of Immigration' enclosed in Keith-Roach's note to the H.C., 28.11.21, I.S.A. 2/218.

[31] Keith-Roach to the H.C., 28.11.21, ibid.

[32] Ibid, ibid.

[33] Churchill to Samuel, 9.3.22, confidential despatch, I.S.A. 2/219.

[34] Samuel to Churchill, 19.4.22, confidential despatch, ibid.

[35] Samuel to Churchill, 27.7.22, despatch 534, C.O.733/23 file 39366.

[36] See minutes of the Economy Committee of the meetings held on 21.10.22, and 8.11.22, enclosed in Samuel's despatch to the Duke of Devonshire, Colonial Secretary, 5.1.23, despatch 17, C.O.733/41 file 262.

[37] Morris to the Treasurer, Palestine Government, 11.10.22, to the Chief Secretary, 20.11.22, and 16.12.22, enclosed in Samuel's despatch of 5.1.23, ibid.

[38] See copies of letters from Italian and French Consuls General in Jerusalem to H.C., enclosed in Samuel's despatch 591 of 10.8.22, F.O. 372/1918 file T10239/147/388; also C.O. to H.C., 28.9.22, despatch 1126, F.O. 372/1918 file T11387/147/388.

[39] See Morris's Report on his tour to immigration centres in Europe, 18.8.21, 733/6 file 47584.

[40] Shuckburgh, minutes, 31.1.23, C.O.733/41 file 2626.

[41] Weizmann, during a meeting with the H.C. in Jerusalem, 5.12.22, C.Z.A. Z4/16146.

[42] Samuel to Devonshire, 13.4.23, despatch 333, C.O.733/44 file 20325.

[43] See note 40 above.

[44] Devonshire to Samuel, 16.5.23, despatch 554, C.O.733/44 file 20325.

[45] Samuel to Devonshire, 1.6.23, confidential despatch C.O.733/45 file 29427.

[46] E. Keith-Roach, minutes, see note 4 above.

[47] Shuckburgh, minutes, 21.7.23, C.O.733/47 file 34189.

[48] See note 47 above; see also notes of 'Discussions between Middle East Department and Sir H. Samuel', 26.7.23, C.O.733/54 file 33324; Shuckburgh to Clayton, Chief Secretary (since March 1923) 26.7.23, confidential despatch, C.O.733/47 file 34189.

[49] See note 47 above; also Sir J. Masterton-Smith, Under Secretary,C.O., minutes, 21.7.23, C.O.733/47 file 34189; 'Extracts of Minutes of Discussion with Sir H. Samuel', 10.7.23, ibid.

[50] F. Kisch to the Political Secretary, Z.O. London, 5.10.23, C.Z.A., Z4/16085.

[51] Samuel to Thomas, Colonial Secretary, 23.5.24, C.O.733/68 file 26356.

[52] A.M. Hyamson to Chief Secretary, 18.5.24, 'confidential' enclosed copy in Samuel's confidential despatch to Thomas, 2.5.24, C.O.733/68 file 22627.

[53] Samuel to Thomas, 23.5.24, see note 51 above.

[54] E. Keith-Roach, minutes, see note 4 above.

[55] Morris to the Treasurer and the Chief Secretary, see note 37 above.

Chapter Six

THE IMMIGRATION ORDINANCE, 1925

THE CAMPAIGN OVER THE IMMIGRATION SCHEME

The lessons of the May Disturbances strengthened the Zionists' original belief that the foundations of the Jewish National Home should be built upon selective and well-controlled immigration. Accordingly, the Zionist diplomatic campaign in London during the second half of 1921 was primarily concerned with regaining their exclusive control over selected immigration. A considerable achievement on this issue was reached at the Immigration Conference in November 1921, when the Colonial Office approved in principle a re-establishment of the 'guaranteed system' under the auspices of the Zionist Organisation. This consent obliged the Colonial Office to include the Zionist Executive in the outlining of new immigration policy with a special view to the control of labour immigration.[1]

Following this agreement, the Colonial Office drafted its proposed scheme of control in accordance with main Zionist demands. The scheme recommended the creation of quarterly immigration quotas — Labour Schedules, agreed and approved by both the Palestine Administration and the Palestine Zionist Executive. Immigrants within these quotas were classified into two categories: the existing category 'E' of skilled and unskilled labour, selected and guaranteed by the Zionist Organisation, and a new category 'H' — members of professions and limited means of independence recommended but not guaranteed by the Organisation.[2]

The Colonial Office submitted the proposed scheme to the Zionist Executive for observation prior to its being sent to the High Commissioner for his approval.[3] Dr. Weizmann, although generally satisfied with the British proposals, asked for more flexibility in the definitions of the new categories and in the allocation of immigration certificates among the various Palestine Offices, in order to make the system 'more workable in practice'.[4] The Colonial Office again went a considerable way towards accepting Weizmann's suggestions, made the relevant amendments and only then sent the scheme to Jerusalem.[5]

The Colonial Office proposals, which had made various significant changes in Samuel's original scheme, undoubtedly placed the High Commissioner in a rather difficult position. Samuel was aware that these amendments would be seen in Palestine as a radical departure from the policy he had declared in his Statement of 3rd June, but since he had agreed that the new scheme should be drafted by the Colonial Office with the participation of the Zionist Executive,[6] he was unable to reject it absolutely. Therefore, in order to reconcile any divergences, the High Commissioner asked the Colonial Office to avoid any formal changes in his original classification (such as the addition of a new category 'H') but nevertheless he agreed to the most essential proposal of creating a Labour Schedule, which would include all immigrants selected and guaranteed by the Zionist Organisation as part of category 'E' — labour. Moreover, in response to local Zionist pressure, he agreed to extend the Schedule period from three to six months and to empower the Palestine Zionist Executive to send the allocation of the Schedule directly to its offices in Europe.[7]

Samuel's agreement in principle with the Labour Schedule gave the Colonial Office the green light for formulating the new scheme in more detailed and concrete form. The scheme, an elaboration of the Zionists' demands within the limits of Samuel's policy, was based on five principles, or rather, five phases in the following order:

1. A bi-annual conference of Palestine Zionist Executive and Palestine Administration. Agreement reached on quotas of guaranteed and non-guaranteed immigrants, trades to which they should belong and allocation to various countries.
2. Immigration Inspectors, British Consuls and Palestine (Zionist) Offices be informed of this agreement.
3. Palestine Offices forward list of selected immigrants, both guaranteed and non-guaranteed, to Immigration Inspectors.
4. Immigration Inspectors to make sure that these candidates really are suitable from economic, health and political points of view.
5. Consuls will grant visas to all immigrants approved by the Inspectors.[8]

This scheme, apart from being designed with a view to 'constructive work in Palestine' and 'necessary to the economic conditions' of the country was, as far as the Colonial Office was concerned, also essential 'to enhance the status . . . and confer a large measure of responsibility' upon the Zionist Organisation, whose control over immigration 'had so much declined as to be practically negligible'. Furthermore, responding to Zionist pressure, the Colonial Secretary could find 'no reason why' this scheme should not be enforced at once, even before the establishment of the Immigration Committee which might have dealt with the 'existing regulations as they stand'.[9]

Meanwhile, taking the Colonial Office proposals into consideration, the Palestine Administration drafted its own scheme. Yet, influenced by the present high rate of unemployment and the inefficient control exerted by British Consuls, the Palestine Administration proposed a stricter scheme which minimised the role of the Zionist Organisation. These proposals were based on four main principles:

1. Determination of a quarterly Schedule by the Palestine Government according to figures presented by its competent Departments and 'with the advice of the Palestine Zionist Executive'.

2. Allocation of the Schedule in quotas and under 'general industrial headings' to the centres of immigration.
3. Primary selection by the Zionist Organisation and other 'approved bodies'.
4. Final selection by Palestine Immigration Officers from amongst the Zionist candidates and 'independent applicants'.[10]

The most significant differences between the two schemes lay in the role delegated to the Zionist Organisation over control of selected immigrants. While the Colonial Office suggested 'an agreement' with the Zionists on rationing and allocation of the Schedule, the High Commissioner proposed that the Palestine Zionist Executive 'would be consulted'. London had granted an exclusive privilege of selection to the Zionist Organisation whereas Jerusalem made it possible for 'other approved bodies' to select and recommend candidates, while final selection was to remain in the hands of the Immigration Inspectors. Nevertheless, as a result of the unofficial agreement between Morris and the Palestine Zionist Executive,[11] the Palestine Administration recommended the formation of an 'indefinite' Labour Pool consisting of unemployed immigrants.

The differences between the proposals of the Colonial Office and the Palestine Administration corresponded to a large extent with the different approaches of the two parts of the Zionist Executive in London and Jerusalem, as well as with their unequal ability to persuade the British to accept their demands. The principal motive of the Zionist Executive in London was the complete restoration of the previous Certificate System which enabled the Zionist Organisation 'to exercise a measure of effective control corresponding to its responsibility'.[12] The Palestine scheme was criticised by the Zionist Executive from a practical as well as a moral point of view. The Executive stated that the Palestine Government lacked sufficient information to enable it to allocate the immigration certificates among the various immigration centres, a matter which the local Zionist Offices 'are far better qualified to deal with'. In particular, the Schedule was to be classified under 'general industrial headings', a condition which needed the proper machinery for selection.[13]

Regarding the proposed appointment of Immigration Officers in several immigration centres in Europe, the Executive re-emphasised its predictions about obvious 'hardships', 'delay' and 'distress' that might be imposed on applicants compelled to travel long distances and waste time and money in order to obtain their visas. Moreover, applicants living outside the 'inspectors' scope' had, according to the proposed scheme, to be referred to Palestine, a procedure which might cause 'serious inconvenience' and 'discouragement' to many candidates for immigration. These difficulties, as far as the Executive was concerned, could be largely obviated by the acceptance of its proposal, in which the Palestine Offices would be allowed to submit their candidates, as under the previous Certificate System, to the Consuls, who would grant visas within the prescribed limit of the Schedule.

Apart from general criticism of the revised scheme, the Zionist Executive suggested numerous specific amendments regarding the definitions of the categories of immigrants. The intention of these amendments was to encourage immigration of a 'creative element' belonging particularly to the middle class. These mainly affected the definition of category 'B' (persons of independent means), category 'H' (persons with limited means of the craftsmen and shopkeeper class), and category 'C' (members of learned professions).

By its counter-proposals the Zionist Executive was not only working in the interests of immigrants, and to increase immigration by any means, but rather towards a more substantial goal — the consolidation of its own position as an exclusively recognised body for selection and regulation of immigration into Palestine. Under Samuel's proposals all immigrants were to be on an equal footing, whether recommended by the Zionist Organisation, by any other 'approved bodies' or not recommended at all. In other words, no special status of any kind was accorded to the Zionist Organisation, 'but on the other hand', the Zionist Executive pointed out, 'public opinion [would] continue to hold the Zionist Organisation responsible for all Jewish immigrants, whether arriving under its auspices or not'. This abnormal situation would render the Organisation unable in any way to limit the nominations of candidates by 'irresponsible bodies', while it would still remain under a 'moral obligation' to provide for them if they failed to make good. Although the Executive did not ask that all immigrants without exception should require a recommendation from the Zionist Organisation, it did insist on having 'special status' of control over selection of labour immigration. Otherwise, it predicted, 'the Organisation's prestige, its power of control and its ability to organise immigration in a systematic manner will be seriously prejudiced'.[14]

The Zionist criticisms and counter-proposals were carefully considered at the Colonial Office, and later transmitted to the Foreign Office and the Home Office to be discussed together at an Inter-Departmental Conference on immigration, to take place in mid-August 1922. The division of opinion among Foreign Office officials prior to that conference illustrates the controversial nature of this question. Major Spencer, for example, supported the High Commissioner's scheme and opposed any concession to be made to the Zionist Organisation which would inevitably weaken the status of the Immigration Officers. In his opinion the Zionist fear that their position would be weakened was 'true, necessary and desirable'. Forbes Adam and Parkin, on the other hand, expressed sympathy with the Zionist demands. Forbes Adam held the view that since the Zionist Organisation held a recognised position in the Mandate itself and had 'borne all the burden and criticism for its success or lack of success, it would be only fair to leave to them as much responsibility as possible in selecting and guaranteeing immigrants'. Parkin, who found that the Zionist proposals 'contain much wisdom from the practical point of view' shared Forbes Adam's observations.[15] However, these views in fact did not have any real bearing on the conference itself. Major Young of the Colonial Office, leading the discussion, explained how far his Office was prepared to go towards meeting the Zionist criticisms, but preferred to leave the actual revision of the scheme to a separate meeting with Batterbee, the representative of the Home Office, and himself.[16]

The results of that meeting could not have been too palatable to the Zionists. Disregarding the political implications of the question, the Young-Batterbee Committee couched its proposals in purely administrative terms. Accordingly, it was suggested that the determination and the allocation of the Schedule be left in the hands of the Palestine Government. Likewise, the recommendation was made that final selection of immigrants should rest in the hands of the Government working through the Immigration Officers, who must be given 'very wide powers to reject the nominees of the Organisation'. In this manner, Zionist fears that they would be held responsible and criticised if undesirables enter Palestine, would be 'unfounded'.[17]

The revised Colonial Office formula, however, did not go so far as to relieve the Zionist Organisation of any participation in actual control over the Schedule. Favouring the Zionist demands, the new scheme recommended the constitution of a Jewish Immigration Bureau in Palestine, which would be consulted before determining the Schedule and would have the power to classify and allocate the immigration certificates according to countries of origin. Following the High Commissioner's provisional approval the Schedule would be submitted to the proposed Palestine Immigration Committee. On the application of the majority of the Committee the question would be referred to the Secretary of State, whose decision would be final.[18]

The revised scheme of the Colonial Office, based on a compromise between the Zionist Executive and Samuel's proposals, might have had a good chance of being approved by both parties, if the Palestine Zionist Executive had not rejected it outright. The draft of the scheme, which was transmitted to the Palestine Government for observation, was leaked to the Palestine Executive, apparently by Morris. The rumours that the Zionist Executive in London was in agreement with these proposals caused angry reaction from the Palestine Executive. Protesting to London, the Zionist Executive in Jerusalem revealed the considerable support they had already gained for their cause from Morris and Norman Bentwich, the Legal Secretary, and the probable damage that London's 'agreement' had done to their diplomatic achievements in Palestine. According to the Palestine Zionist Executive, Morris and Bentwich were of the opinion that the new proposals were 'even more restrictive than the regulation at present in force, and certainly not so broad as the Immigration Department would like to see them'. Morris himself, the Palestine Zionist Executive claimed, was ready to recommend the creation of a considerable Labour Pool, to limit the control of Immigration Inspectors to questions of health and political conviction only, and to approve a schedule of 20,000 (!) immigrants for the following year — a figure on which he had based his administrative budget.[19]

In addition to their complaints, the Palestine Executive sent to London a long memorandum criticising the revised scheme and presenting their own proposals. In their opinion, the Colonial Office scheme was based on two wrong assumptions. First, that Jewish economic development in Palestine would necessarily be confined to agriculture, whereas industrial and commercial development would certainly afford much more room for immigration than could agriculture. Second, that society in Palestine was regarded in the scheme as both 'mechanical and static' and that the 'creative faculty' of immigration was disregarded. The Palestine Executive emphasised that Jewish immigrants did 'not merely fit actually vacant posts but were the creative factors who increased the whole wealth of the community, who discover the new sources and forms of production and who not only employ themselves but create employment for others'.[20]

This theory found concrete expression in the Palestine Zionist Executive counter-proposals, by requesting that immigration be facilitated for persons of independent means and those who intended to follow their academic and professional calling in Palestine. The principal issue, however, remained the maintenance of the Labour Pool consisting of immigrants coming under category 'E'. The Palestine Executive emphasised the economic advantages of a certain amount of unemployment in the country, which in its opinion was 'necessary in order to render possible development in industry, commerce and agriculture and also to secure a proper relation between wages and capital' — in other words, to assure a constant supply of Jewish labour irrespective of the existing demand for labour. At the same time, the Executive made it clear that its demand for the Pool was, in fact, only an alternative if the Government would not accept the 'wider principle' of the Certificate System.[21]

Despite this statement, it seems quite obvious that at this stage the Palestine Executive gave first priority to the Labour Pool, which in the short term could offer a better alleviation for its political and financial distress.[22]

The sharp criticism and proposals coming from the Palestine Executive apparently surprised and embarrasssed the London Zionist Executive. The differences of opinion between London and Jerusalem Zionists appeared serious. S. Finkelstein, the former Secretary for Immigration of the Central Zionist Office in London, who was invited to examine these differences, suggested that it would not be difficult to adjust the London policy to the one suggested by Jerusalem. Generally in favour of the Palestine Zionist Executive proposals, he recommended that they be adopted when negotiations with the Colonial Office were resumed.[23] The Zionist Executive, however, thought differently. Insisting on full uniformity of the Zionist stands both in London and Jerusalem, the Executive dictated to Jerusalem their principles as follows:

1. Restoration of the guaranteed Certificate System and rejection of the Labour Pool as a basic determination of the Schedule.
2. The Zionist Organisation to be the 'sole Agency' entitled to introduce guaranteed immigrants and allocate the certificates to the various centres of emigration.
3. Rejection of the appointment of Immigration Inspectors.
4. British Passport Officers to be authorised to reject

Zionist nominees on 'special political grounds' only, and the visa they grant should be 'definite and final'.
5. Drastic reduction of visa fees for immigrants to Palestine.[24]

Careful examination of the so-called 'differences of opinion' between the two parts of the Zionist Executive does not reveal disagreements of much significance. The dispute really lay in mutual distrust and rivalry as well as in differences in emphasis and tactics. The Palestine Executive, well aware of its financial and political limits, preferred to act more pragmatically towards solving its most acute problems. Its persistent demand for a Labour Pool was designed to increase Jewish immigration by all possible means, even beyond the actual needs of the country for labour. The Zionist Executive, on the other hand, acting more dogmatically towards a long-range settlement, did not give up its principal demand for restoration of the Certificate System. Its main object was to achieve as much control as possible, in order to regulate immigration according to its own decision.

Weizmann's visit to Palestine at the end of 1922 offered a suitable opportunity to co-ordinate and unify the Zionist stands. A few sessions of the Palestine Executive, with representatives of the Jewish National Council and Weizmann present, were devoted to the immigration question. Most of the speakers justified the Labour Pool by describing its advantages from both economic and political points of view. Considering the impending formation of the Immigration Committee they expressed their fears that the Schedule would be open to constant Arab opposition and might frequently be postponed, if the proposed procedure of referring it to the Secretary of State were to be implemented. On the other hand, the administration of the Pool could be set up without the need to consult the Arabs. Dr. Weizmann, on the other hand, advocating the adoption of the London Executive policy, placed himself in the minority.[25]

Since the assembly could not reach a unanimous decision it was suggested that an ad hoc committee be nominated out of the Executive and the Council, whose duty would be to outline a programme on which further negotiations with the

Government would be based. Characteristically, the ad hoc committee adopted a Resolution which included both schemes; namely, to obtain a Labour Pool of 3,000 unemployed but at the same time to allow a continuous flow of 500 'guaranteed' immigrants per month under category 'E', irrespective of the Pool. Nevertheless, as the Committee felt that its far-reaching demand might not be accepted by the Government, it proposed a detailed bargaining retreat from its original proposal, whose final phase was a Schedule of 12,000 guaranteed immigrants per annum.[26]

Furnished with that resolution a strong Zionist delegation including Dr. Weizmann and Colonel Frederick Kisch, the new Chairman-designate of the Palestine Zionist Executive, met Samuel and senior Palestine officials to discuss the entire immigration question. Colonel Kisch opened the discussion by presenting the Zionist demands. Dr. Weizmann added that a considerable margin of unemployed was not only favourable in a sense to Jewish interests, 'but also a healthy economic agent' for the country. Basing his arguments only on the economic advantages of their proposals, Dr. Weizmann stated that he was anxious to establish a system which could allow a regular influx of immigrants without the present 'artificial, inelastic and over-classified' scheme. In his view, 'a more generous and comprehensive policy would stimulate and increase effort and capital, with a satisfactory reaction upon the capacity of the country to absorb immigration'.[27]

Zionist criticism and proposals found considerable support among some of the British officials present at the meeting. Wyndham Deedes, the Chief Secretary, Morris and Colonel Solomon, the Director of Commerce and Industry, agreed that there were at present 'too many restrictions on immigration' and that the Schedule was 'an artificial method'. They recommended that the Zionist Organisation should be allowed to maintain a large Labour Pool and introduce guaranteed immigrants 'on broad lines according to the immediate state of economic affairs'.

Hyamson, however, in defence of Government policy, contradicted his colleagues by arguing that the existing scheme had 'failed' or 'proved itself ineffective'. Describing as 'somewhat exaggerated' the Zionist claims that unskilled Jewish workmen showed great adaptability for skilled trades, he insisted on the need for classifying the Schedule into trades. Furthermore, he rejected the Zionist demand for exclusivity in introducing immigrants and urged that the Schedule should also provide room for individuals, non-Jews and non-Zionists, which could apply directly to the British authorities.

Samuel, of the opinion that immigration had not, so far as experience showed, kept pace with the 'capacity of the country to absorb new arrivals', rejected the Zionist demands which he considered even more contradictory to that principle. Admitting that the attempts to base the extent of immigration on 'strict arithmetical calculations' had been disappointing, the High Commissioner suggested basing the Schedule 'only upon existing economic factors'.[28]

This all-round criticism of the unsatisfactory results of the existing immigration scheme eventually brought the High Commissioner to the conclusion that the new scheme should not be so 'rigid' and 'meticulous'. Submitting his new general observations to the Colonial Office, Samuel stated that it was 'not practical of course to exercise so minute a control that every individual immigrant . . . can be co-ordinated with a particular vacancy'. 'Jewish labour', he pointed out, 'is found to possess adaptability in a high degree and very many men who belong to one calling when they first arrive, are found in quite different occupations later.' The High Commissioner recommended therefore that the Schedule be determined more frequently — every three months, fixed only six weeks in advance, and extended during its execution if necessary. Likewise, he suggested various amendments to the definitions of the immigration categories in order to achieve 'much elasticity and common sense'.[29]

However, since the High Commissioner had not yet revealed his intentions to the Palestine Executive and the despatch containing his proposals somehow did not reach London until the middle of January 1923, there had been much understandable uneasiness in Zionist circles in Jerusalem and London.[30] This excitement was not only a result of speculations on Samuel's future policy, but derived mainly from the fear that the new scheme would not be operational before the constitution of the proposed Immigration Committee. The Zionist Executive in London was at pains to convince the Colonial Office 'that the argumentative position of the Palestine Government vis-a-vis the Immigration Committee, will be considerably strengthened if the Committee, when it meets, finds a well considered scheme already in operation'.[31] These developments placed the Zionist Executive in a race against the clock, as the appointed time of the Legislative Council elections came nearer and nearer.

The decisive initiative eventually came from Dr. Weizmann. Submitting the Zionists' final proposals, Weizmann notified Shuckburgh of his impending visit to the U.S.A. and his anxiety to settle the immigration question before his departure. He maintained that his prospect of success in America would be 'very materially improved' if the immigration question could be disposed of.[32]

The anticipated conference at the Colonial Office which took place a few days later went 'far to satisfy' the Zionists. In many respects it was a successful repetition of the fateful Immigration Conference at the Colonial Office in November 1921 and further evidence of Weizmann's diplomatic talent. The list of the Zionist achievements following that Conference was a long and 'very impressive one', at least as far as the Zionist Executive was concerned:

1. General approval of the restoration of the Certificate system for 'guaranteed' immigrants by the Zionist Organisation.
2. The 'guarantee' was limited for one year only.
3. Determination of the Labour Schedule every six months.
4. Allocation of the Schedule by the Zionist Organisation with final approval of the Palestine Government.
5. Reduction of the minimum capital required for visas for craftsmen and artisans, from £500 to £200 only.
6. Admission of students and orphans, providing evidence of sufficient means for maintenance.

    7. Extension of category 'D' — dependants, to include
       fiancées.[33]

Nevertheless, the Zionist Executive had to admit that its
efforts to postpone the appointment of Immigration
Inspectors ended with failure. The Inspectors, in spite of
Zionist protests, were authorised to examine the political as
well as economic and health suitability of all immigrants and
to reject even those recommended and guaranteed by the
Zionist Organisation.[34]

LEGISLATION OF THE ORDINANCE

The Colonial Office revised Draft, embodying the
Agreement reached at the Immigration Conference of
February 1923, was first presented to the Zionist Executive
and then despatched to Jerusalem. It was anticipated at the
Colonial Office that the Draft, as it had been revised in
London, would take immediate effect in the form of new
Regulations, with no further modifications. According to the
original schedule, the Draft should have been submitted to
the Immigration Committee for approval, as soon as that
body was constituted.[35] However, since the elections for the
Legislative Council had been heavily boycotted, the whole
scheme was postponed.

    Nevertheless, the Immigration Department took
advantage of this delay to consult other branches of the
Palestine Administration. The circulars sent to all District
Governors and the Directors of Commerce and Industry,
Police, Labour and Health sought 'urgent' observations
concerning the new Regulations. But since the Draft was
considered confidential and thus not attached to these
appeals, these bodies had very little to suggest at that stage.[36]
This amounted only to the Police's request that provisions be
made for detaining persons recommended for deportation,
and a request from the Director of Health that medical certificates be forwarded in advance with the original application, in order to reduce deportations on medical grounds.[37]

    Norman Bentwich, the Legal Secretary, who was invited to
convert the scheme into Regulations, made numerous
amendments in the Draft. Those were designed to ensure

unequivocal interpretation and to avoid loopholes and mis-understandings of the law, but without affecting its flexibility. Accordingly, he suggested determining the age at which orphans (Category 'A iv') would reach independent maintenance; to specify precisely the minimum capital for artisans (Category 'A ii') in each trade, but at the same time not to limit persons of independent means (Category 'A i') to investing their capital in one particular branch. Nevertheless, these stricter definitions of the law's clauses inevitably reduced the power of discretion of the Immigration Department.[38]

Although Bentwich was careful not to interfere with any political aspects of the law, his proposition to omit from the Regulations all sections dealing with functions of Consuls, Immigration Inspectors and the Palestine Offices in regard to actual control was extremely significant. Since these matters were considered as 'administrative' and not 'legal', it was suggested they be dealt with separately by direct communication with the bodies concerned.[39] This arrangement could enable the Government to act more freely and to co-ordinate its policy according to the economic and political circumstances in Palestine. In this manner, actual control over immigration policy could also be excluded from the authority of any legislative body which might be constituted.[40]

The new Draft Regulations were issued in accordance with Article 11 of the 'Immigration Ordinance, 1920', which authorised the Director of Immigration, with the approval of the High Commissioner, 'to issue from time to time any order and regulations for the better control of immigration into Palestine'. The Palestine Government was at that time of the opinion that the amendment of the Immigration Ordinance itself 'must await the constitution of a legislative body'[41] which the Administration was still hoping to form.

The Draft endeavoured to preserve the spirit of the Colonial Office's final scheme by adopting in general its definitions of the immigration categories and the principles of the Labour Schedule.[42] The only amendment which might be considered significant was the proposition to limit the extension of the Schedule during its execution to 10 per cent or 300 immigrants whichever be the greater number.[43] This provision was approved by the Colonial Office, but under further pressure of the High Commissioner the extension of the Schedule was reduced to 5 per cent only.[44]

Nevertheless, the separate 'communiqué' to be directed to the Palestine Zionist Executive, which was probably drafted by Hyamson, went further in reducing the Zionist demands as approved by the Colonial Office. Outlining the proposed role of the Zionist Organisation in the actual execution of the Schedule, the Palestine Government insisted that 'consultations' with the Palestine Executive would take place only after its provisional determination and not before. Moreover, the Executive was only entitled to put forward its own proposals for 'completing vacancies in the Schedule' after the Administration had considered applications for certificates from private employers, who applied directly to the Immigration Department.[45] Thus, the Zionist Organisation lost its superiority regarding the Labour Schedule, as agreed in the Immigration Conference of February 1923.

The unemployment crisis in Palestine, which reached a peak in the summer of 1923 and was accompanied by a drastic drop in immigration and increase of emigration, decreased the urgency for new Regulations. Due to these circumstances and with the absence of substantial Zionist pressure to speed up the legislation process, the drafting of the Immigration Regulations moved very slowly. Ultimately the Regulations were sanctioned two years later, under a new Immigration Ordinance.

This long delay began in Palestine. The Legal Secretary sent the first Draft Regulations to London after a delay of three months. They were sent back to him by the Colonial Office after a further delay of two months to be re-drafted, 'in order to bring them into conformity with the usual style and requirements of a legal enactment'. Nevertheless, the Secretary of State authorised Samuel to publish the substance of the new Scheme as a Public Notice, if he considered the matter urgent.[46] Contrary to the view of the Legal Secretary, who recommended immediate approval of the Regulations,[47] Samuel preferred to wait and to issue them as a legislative enactment.[48] Apart from excluding Palestinian citizens and travellers from the Regulations and consequently relettering the categories, the revised Draft was returned to London without any substantial amendments.[49] However, three months later, a new Draft outlined by Hyamson, now acting Director of Immigration, reached the Colonial Office accompanied by an urgent appeal for its 'early approval'.[50]

After careful examination of the latest Draft and its co-ordination with the existing Ordinance, the Colonial Office came to the conclusion that not only would it be necessary to redraft the Regulations completely, but also that the Regulations could not be put into satisfactory shape unless the Immigration Ordinance itself were amended.[51] This conclusion launched a new round of consultations in the spring of 1924, on the initiative of the Colonial Office.

The drafting of the new Ordinance and Regulations was conducted by Gerald Clauson, who had specialised in the immigration question of Palestine and had most of the previous Colonial Office proposals to his credit.[52] Clauson took advantage of the presence of Nathan Mindel, the acting Director of the Immigration Department, who happened to be in London on vacation, and consulted him and Edward Keith-Roach, the former Assistant Secretary of the Palestine Government who, according to a rotation system, had been transferred to the Colonial Office. The participation of Mindel and Keith-Roach, who were well acquainted with all the aspects of immigration, ensured that the Palestine point of view would be considered and expressed accordingly in the law.

It seems quite obvious that the main motive of the new Ordinance, in comparison with the previous one, was to make control over immigration as strict and efficient as possible.[53] This policy was quite plainly expressed in the measures provided, to prevent any arrival or entry of irregular cases as well as to facilitate and accelerate their deportation, if necessary. To this end, the list of persons not to be permitted entry was significantly lengthened, and included among others also 'unsuitable persons' without specifying any concrete reason (5a).[54] Likewise, the list of reasons for deportation was extended to include further reasons which did not appear in the first Ordinance (8c, 8d, 8e, 8f). In order to facilitate deportations, every immigrant had to possess a valid passport or other document establishing his nationality to make his repatriation, if necessary, possible (5g). In addition, the law of limitation for the purpose of deportation had been revoked.

The Colonial Office revised Regulations emphasised the stricter definition of the law. This stood out in particular in the redivision of the immigration categories. The category of 'Persons of Independent Means' (old 'B')[55], for example, was divided into four new categories, ('A'$_1$, 'A'$_2$, 'A'$_3$, and 'B'). 'Dependants' on individuals or institutions in Palestine (old 'D') were redivided into three new categories ('A'$_4$, 'A'$_6$, and 'D'), while in practice new 'D' itself was subdivided into six sub-categories ('A'$_{1(2)}$, 'A'$_{2(2)}$, 'A'$_{3(2)}$, 'A'$_{4(2)}$, 'B'$_2$, and 'C'$_2$.

By the middle of July 1924, the amended Ordinance, accompanied by revised Regulations and Instructions to His Majesty's Consuls and Passport Control Officers, were sent simultaneously to the Palestine Government, the Zionist Executive, and the Foreign and Home Offices for observation.[56]

The Foreign and the Home Offices came to similar conclusions. Both indirectly criticised the complicated character of the scheme by pointing out the 'heavy' and 'unconventional' tasks imposed upon the British representatives abroad.[57]

The Zionist Executive, which this time had not been consulted during the preliminary drafting of the law, submitted a long memorandum, including numerous observations and proposals. Their criticism focused round the changes mentioned above, i.e. the question of passports, the various disqualifications for entry and the proposed procedure for deportation. Contrary to the view of the Foreign and Home Offices, they recommended that decisions be left to the discretion of the Consuls, in order to reduce the necessity for frequent referral of cases to Jerusalem. Regarding deportation of irregular or 'unsuitable persons', it was suggested that such cases should be confined to appropriate Courts in order to avoid miscarriage of justice.

The main Zionist criticism, however, lay with the new Regulations which gave legal interpretation to the scheme agreed and approved by them at the Immigration Conference of February 1923. That scheme, meanwhile, had felt the consequences of the grave economic situation in Palestine and the consequences of Arab non-co-operation. Now presenting their observations, the Executive made desperate efforts to turn back the clock and bridge the considerable gap between that agreement and the new law. To this end they based their argument on the moral obligation of the Colonial Office, in view of its promises and agreement, as well as on the recent economic improvement in Palestine which might substantially strengthen their bargaining stand.[58]

No less radical and comprehensive were the observations made by Hyamson, the newly appointed Controller of Immigration. They were concentrated on three main objectives: to make control more effective and efficient, to reduce its cost and to increase its revenue as much as possible. As far as he was concerned, the Regulations went 'far too much into detail and dealt with matters of internal machinery' that ought to be left to the officers administering the control. As it had been constructed, 'the machinery could not work and control would come to a standstill'. However, an attempt to apply the Regulations would impose a large amount of additional work on the Consuls as well as the Permits Section and must increase materially the cost of control. At the same time, the numerous difficulties and delays placed in the way of immigrants would inevitably reduce their numbers and affect the revenue of the Permits Section.[59]

Accordingly, he suggested extending the functions of his Section and increasing the powers of discretion imposed on the British Consuls, in order to avoid unnecessary references and correspondence between them. In more concrete terms: to authorise the Consuls to grant visas to Palestine residents and immigrants with capital, without having to refer to Jerusalem; to simplify the system of allocation and distribution of Immigration Certificates, whereby they should be issued locally according to general authorisation from Jerusalem; to reduce entry of unsuitable and irregular cases by production of health certificates in advance and introducing stricter examination by Consuls; and finally, to speed up deportation procedure in order to prevent extra expenses and risks of escape.[60]

Emphasising his practical knowledge and long experience, contrary to the 'theoretical acquaintances' of those who drafted the law in London, Hyamson pressed vigorously for adoption of his own observations.[61] To this end, he very greatly desired to be sent urgently to London to take part in the final drafting of the Ordinance.[62] However, Samuel did not give much backing to Hyamson's proposals, not did he agree to his sudden visit to London.[63] Without Samuel's approval, Hyamson's proposed amendments had very slim chances of being considered by the Colonial Office.[64]

The new Immigration Ordinance was eventually published in September 1925, and came into force one month later, without being significantly affected, either by Zionist criticism or by Hyamson's proposals.[65]

NOTES

[1] See Chapter 3, p. 50.

[2] See the first draft of the scheme enclosed in Churchill's confidential despatch to Samuel, 14.12.21, C.O.733/16, file 58536.

[3] Shuckburgh to Weizmann, 6.12.21, ibid.

[4] Weizmann to Shuckburgh, 7.12.21, ibid.

[5] Shuckburgh to Weizmann, 12.12.21, ibid., see note 2 above.

[6] Samuel to Churchill, tel. 405, 4.10.21, C.O.733/16 file 49714.

[7] Wyndham Deedes, Acting H.C., to Churchill, tel. 521, 30.12.21, C.O.733/8 file 245; see draft of that telegram in I.S.A. 11/6.

[8] The scheme was drafted by Eric Mills, C.O., 2.2.22, C.O.733/18 file 4741; see also Shuckburgh's minutes, of the same date, ibid.

[9] Churchill to Samuel, confidential despatch, 21.3.22, C.O.733/36 file 11723. Regarding the proposals of setting up an Immigration Committee, see Chapter 4, pp. 72-3.

[10] Deedes to Churchill, confidential despatch, 10.3.22, C.O.733/19 file 13505.

[11] See Chapter 4, pp. 69-70.

[12] Leonard Stein, Political Secretary, C.Z.O., London, to Under Secretary of State, C.O., 10.3.22, C.O.733/36 file 11723.

[13] See 'Immigration to Palestine', memorandum by Z.E., London, 19.6.22, C.Z.A., S6/276; also in C.O.733/36 file 29685.

[14] Ibid, ibid.

[15] See minutes of Major Spencer, Eastern Department, F.O., 3.8.22, Forbes Adam, 3.8.22, and R.T. Parkin 4.8.22, both of Treaty Department, F.O., F.O.372/1917 file T8965/147/388.

[16] See minutes of that Conference, 14.8.22, F.O. 372/1918 file T9643/147/388.

[17] H. Young's minutes to E. Mills, undated, C.O.733/31 file 39243; also notes by Forbes Adam on conversation with Young, 24.8.22, F.O. 372/1918 file T9892/147/388.

[18] See 'Scheme for Control of Immigration into Palestine', 7.9.22, in F.O. 372/1918 file T10876/147/388.

[19] See 'extract from a letter . . .' P.Z.E. to Z.E., 18.9.22; also 'extract from note of interview . . .' with the H.C. 17.9.22, both enclosed in Leonard Stein's letter to E. Mills, 6.10.22, C.O.733/36, file 4999.

[20] P.Z.E. 'Memorandum on Immigration', 21.9.22, I.S.A. 11/6.

[21] Ibid, ibid.

[22] See Chapter 4 p. 69.

[23] 'Memorandum' by S. Finkelstein, 10.10.22, C.Z.A. L3/31.

[24] S. Finkelstein to P.Z.E., 23.11.22, 'confidential', ibid.

[25] P.Z.E., Minutes of meeting, 1.12.22, C.Z.A., unclassified.

[26] Minutes of meeting, 3.12.22, ibid.

[27] See 'Minutes of the Meeting . . . to Consider Questions Relating to Immigration', 5.12.22, C.Z.A. Z4/16146.

[28] Ibid, ibid.

[29] Samuel to Devonshire, 21.12.22, C.O.733/28 file 290.

[30] F. Kisch to Leonard Stein, 9.1.23, Kisch to Stein, 16.1.23, Stein to Kisch 22.1.23; Kisch to Stein, 28.1.23, all in C.Z.A., Z4/16085; also Stein to Kisch 7.2.23, Z4/16129.

[31] Stein to Kisch, 16.1.23, C.Z.A., Z4/16085.

[32] Weizmann to Shuckburgh, 16.2.23, in an attached letter to Z.E.'s memo 'Revised Scheme for the Control of Immigration into Palestine', submitted to C.O., 15.2.23, C.O.733/59 file, 8490; also in C.Z.A., S6/274.

[33] See minutes of Conference, 21.2.23, C.O.733/54 file 9748; copy of the revised scheme in H. Young to Deedes, 1.3.23, S. Finkelstein Z.O., London, to P.Z.E., 27.2.23, C.Z.A., S6/272.

[34] S. Finkelstein to P.Z.E., 15.3.23, ibid.

[35] See 'Notes of Interview with Major Young . . .' by L. Stein, 27.2.23, C.Z.A. S6/275.

[36] See a copy of those circulars, all dated 30.4.23, 11/1/1I.

[37] Deputy Inspector General of Police, 4.5.23, and Director of Health, 16.5.23, both to Director of Immigration and Travel, ibid.

[38] Attorney General to Director of Immigration, 22.7.23, 26.8.23, both ibid.

[39] Ibid, ibid.

[40] See hint for that in G. Clayton, Acting H.C. to Devonshire, 'confidential', 24.8.23, C.O.733/48 file 43844.

[41] Attorney General to Director of Immigration, 22.7.23, I.S.A. 11/1/1I.

[42] See Draft, enclosed in Clayton's confidential despatch 24.8.23, see note 40 above.

[43] Max Nurock, Assistant Secretary, Palestine Government, to Director of Immigration, 18.4.23, I.S.A. 11/6; Samuel to Devonshire, 'confidential', 20.4.23, 11/1/1I.

[44] See minutes of 'Discussion between Middle East Department and Samuel', 26.7.23, C.O.733/54, file 33324.

[45] See draft of proposed communiqué enclosed in Clayton's despatch, note 40 above.

[46] Devonshire to Samuel, 'confidential', 2.10.23, C.O.733/48 file 43844.

[47] Bentwich to Chief Secretary, 18.12.23, I.S.A. 11/1/1I.

[48] Samuel to Devonshire, 'confidential', 21.12.23, C.O.733/52/457.

[49] See revised draft enclosed in Samuel's despatch, ibid.

[50] Enclosed in H.C. to the Secretary of State, 'confidential', 26.3.24, C.O.733/66 file 19618.

[51] E. Keith-Roach to N. Mindel (undated), ibid.

[52] H. Young, Middle East Department in minutes, 11.7.24, C.O.733/86 file 20749.

[53] See first Draft of Ordinance, ibid.

[54] The numbers in brackets show the final numeration of the Articles as they appear in the published Immigration Ordinance, see Palestine *Ordinances,* 1925, p.171.

[55] See Appendices 3 and 4.

[56] See copies of the attached letters dated 16.7.24, in C.O.733/86 file 20749.

[57] See copy of letters from H. Montgomery, F.O. 9.8.24; C.D.C. Robinson, H.O., 14.8.24, both addressed to the Under Secretary of State, Colonial Office, in I.S.A. 11/1/1I.

[58] See Z.O.'s memorandum enclosed in a letter to the Under Secretary of State, 30.7.24, also 27.11.24, ibid.

[59] Hyamson to Chief Secretary, 16.10.24, ibid.

[60] See Hyamson's memorandum, 16.10.24, I.S.A. 11/1/1I; Hyamson to Chief Secretary, 15.1.25, ibid.

[61] See note 59 above.

[62] Hyamson to Chief Secretary, 11.12.24, I.S.A. 11/1/1I.

[63] Max Nurock, acting Chief Secretary, to Hyamson, 21.12.24, ibid.

[64] Roland V. Vernon, Middle East Department, C.O., minutes and memorandum, 13.5.25, C.O.733/92 file 20629.

[65] Compare first Draft, note 53, with published Ordinance, note 54 above.

Chapter Seven

EBB AND FLOW:ECONOMIC ABSORPTIVE CAPACITY AS A CRITERION FOR IMMIGRATION

INAUGURATION OF THE NEW POLICY

The principle of Economic Absorptive Capacity as it appeared in the Statement of 'British Policy in Palestine' (included in the White Paper of June 1922), subsequently became the official credo of the Immigration Department. This principle stated that 'immigration cannot be so great in volume as to exceed whatever may be the economic capacity of the country at the time to absorb new arrivals' and further ensured 'that the immigrants should not be a burden upon the people of Palestine as a whole, and they should not deprive any section of the present population of their employment'.[1]

Samuel, who took an active part in the composition of the Statement and was undoubtedly the author of the principle concerned[2], had already expressed its essence in his own Statement of 3rd June 1921. In fact, the new immigration scheme, first introduced in Samuel's Statement, was based entirely on this principle. The classification of immigrants according to their economic merits was designed to enable the Administration to deal with every category separately and to regulate immigration according to the actual economic and employment needs of the country.[3]

Although the High Commissioner indicated in his Statement that 'the conditions of Palestine are such as do not

117

permit anything in the nature of a mass immigration', there was nothing in the scheme itself to limit immigration numerically, or prevent a mass immigration. Immigrants were able to enter the country as long as they could produce sufficient evidence of independent means for their maintenance, definite prospects of employment or dependence on residents who were in a position to support them. However, the implementation of this policy was a question of interpretation and execution by the machinery of control.

The renewal of immigration according to the revised policy was not followed by an immediate and adequate change in the machinery of control.[4] As before the suspension of May 21, this remained mainly in the hands of the British Consuls. In the absence of direct communication between the Immigration Department and the Consuls, long delays and misinterpretations of the policy were almost inevitable.[5]

Shortly after the announcement of the new policy by Samuel, the Foreign Office informed the Consuls of the new definitions of the immigration categories and instructed them to grant visas accordingly to all immigrants, excepting those under category 'E' — labour.[6] Apparently the principles of the new scheme were not completely understood by the Consuls. What was a definition of 'person of independent means'? What was a 'member of profession'? What constituted a 'dependant'? These were some of the questions raised by the Consuls and passed on to the Colonial Office by the Foreign Office.[7] Due to a lack of further instructions from Jerusalem, Colonial Office officials spent some time on improvisatory interpretations of the Instructions. Gerald Clauson, for example, suggested fixing the minimum capital required for a person of independent means at £500 at least,[8] a qualification which the Palestine Administration approved post factum. However, it appeared that many of the Consuls did not wait for further clarification and granted visas according to their own discretion.[9]

The freedom of discretion granted to the Consuls was not significantly reduced by the new Interim Regulations issued in Palestine in August 1921.[10] The Regulations authorised Consuls to grant visas, without reference to Jerusalem, to travellers ('A') and residents of Palestine ('G') as well as to immigrants with independent means ('B'), persons of religious occupation ('F') and members of professions ('C'). Dependants on residents ('D') and labourers with specified employers ('E') had to be furnished with certificates from the Immigration Department supporting their request for a visa. The necessity for certificates for immigrants coming under categories 'D' and 'E' was apparently not interpreted by the Consuls as indispensable in all cases. At any rate, this was the impression of the Palestine Administration following the arrival of many hundreds of immigrants who did not fulfil the conditions laid down in the Instructions.[11] Nevertheless, a great part of the blame for this state of affairs must be attributed to the indistinct definitions of the categories, which eventually provided the Zionist Commission with a convenient pretext to press for a more lenient interpretation of the Regulations.

Immediately after the issue of the Regulations, the Commission began negotiations with the Administration on this matter. According to an agreement reached with the Zionists in September 1921 the Administration agreed to reduce 'in certain cases' the minimum capital required from persons of independent means from £500 to £120 or a secure income of £6 per month; to allow unrestricted admission of members of professions ('C') provided indubitable evidence of their qualifications could be supplied; and to give a broader interpretation to the definition of dependant or resident ('D'), to include wives, unmarried daughters and sisters without limitation of age, and sons, brothers and apprentices up to 18 years of age.[12] However, Samuel was still firm in his decision not to change the procedure governing admission of labour into the country and insisted that they must be only 'skilled artisans with definite prospects of employment with specific employers.'[13]

Since the capacity of Zionist enterprises in Palestine to provide new jobs for immigrants was very limited, the Palestine Executive was compelled to apply to private employers to come to its aid. The Executive then constituted local committees of private employers, whose task was to provide lists of available vacancies in various Jewish enterprises, in order to obtain immigration certificates for labour. At the same time the Zionist Offices were advised by Jerusalem to ask their fellow countrymen in Palestine to set up similar committees for the same purpose.[14]

Yet, considering the large supply of local labour in Palestine, these measures were unlikely to achieve effective results.[15] The supply of Jewish labour had increased even more by the end of 1921 with the termination of public works in military projects and road construction and the return of Arab labour to Jewish colonies following the political tranquillity which had been interrupted by the May Disturbances.[16] The combination of these factors increased the unemployment rate during spring 1922, which reached an unprecedented record, in March, of 2,500 unemployed, most of them newcomers.[17]

This state of affairs compelled the High Commissioner in March 1922 to introduce drastic measures of control, particularly where labour and 'dependent' immigrants were concerned.[18] These measures were primarily designed to reduce significantly the existing discretionary powers given to the Consuls and to concentrate actual control within the Immigration Department. The Consuls had been instructed to refer to Jerusalem 'all applications for visas under categories 'A', 'B', and 'G'.'[19] In other words, all immigrants except those with independent means had to obtain specific authorisation from the Immigration Department to enter the country. At the same time, the Department itself was instructed to suspend the issue of further permits temporarily 'except in very special cases'.[20]

In this manner immigration was, though unofficially, temporarily suspended. However, the effect of the new method on the actual flow of immigration was neither immediate nor very decisive. Due to lack of direct communication with the Consuls, instructions from Jerusalem were passed to them through the Colonial Office and then the Foreign Office with four weeks' delay.[21] This delay was partly caused by some hesitations at the Colonial Office, which, while negotiating with the Arab Delegation, feared that any suspension might be interpreted by the Arabs as a concession to their recent demand.[22] Eventually the instructions were despatched to the Consuls at the beginning of April, but their effect was not felt in Palestine until June. Although the total volume of immigration fell by over 40 per cent during June-August, in comparison with the preceding quarter,[23] some drop was already anticipated owing to the unfavourable weather conditions during the summer months.[24] More significant, however, was the new distribution of immigration among the various categories. Immigration under category 'E', for example, dropped during the summer quarter from 40 per cent to 20 per cent of the total volume in comparison with that of April,[25] while the volume of 'D' increased from 30 per cent to 50 per cent respectively. This phenomenon was even more significant in September when 'labour' dropped to 15 per cent and 'dependants' rose to 65 per cent of the total volume. This fluctuation was not only proportional but also absolute, since immigration under 'E' dropped from 282 in April to an average of 94 in June-August while immigration under 'D' increased from 222 in April to 265 respectively.

The transition of immigrants from one category to another was an indirect consequence of the inauguration of the Labour Schedule. Since the Schedule limited labour immigration numerically, some legitimate immigrants for category 'E' apparently preferred to apply for visas under category 'D'. This tendency brought about further counter-measures by the Palestine Administration which will be described below, but it is first advisable to consider policy regarding the Schedule.

OPERATION OF THE LABOUR SCHEDULE

Following the Immigration Conference of November 1921, the Colonial Office, in response to Zionist pressure, urged Samuel to restore the former 'ration system' to include all immigrants coming under the auspices of the Zionist Organisation. The Zionist Executive, anxious to extend the Organisation's powers of control, suggested that the approved immigration quotas should include not only labour, but also lower middle class immigrants such as retail shopkeepers, craftsmen and artisans with limited means, all to be selected and regulated by the Organisation.[26] It was thus the Zionists themselves who had been the first to recommend limiting numerically the vast majority of immigrants. Samuel agreed in general to operate a 'ration system', but insisted that all immigrants coming within the quota — labour or others — should come 'under the heading of specific enterprises'.[27] Yet it was understood by all parties concerned that the actual operation of the scheme had to await the enforcement of the new Immigration Regulations, then being drafted.

However, in consequence of the temporary suspension of labour immigration in March 1922 and the revised instructions to Consuls, the Palestine Administration decided on the early inauguration of a Labour Schedule without waiting for the new Regulations to be issued. The early operation of the Schedule system was considered by the Administration as a prompt and adequate measure 'to determine the number and classification of immigrants more accurately'.[28] This decision was welcomed by the Zionist Executive, whose opinion was that 'only with the restoration of that [ration] system and the renewal of definite responsibilities [on the part of the Zionist Organisation] it carries with it, will it become possible for effective and systematic control to be readily exercised'. The Executive emphasised, however, that if they attached importance to the early operation of the Schedule, it was not because they expected or desired to permit any large and immediate increase in the volume of immigration, but merely to enable them to regain the powers of control which they had formerly enjoyed.[29]

The motivation of the Zionist Executive in London was not accepted without appeal by the Palestine Zionist Executive, whose foremost concern was to increase immigration, despite the current unemployment crisis and its very limited means of absorbing further newcomers. Although the Palestine Executive was well aware of the gravity of the economic situation, it could not agree to limit labour immigration numerically. Thus, its proposal for a Labour Pool as an alternative to the Schedule was designed to avoid any immediate correlation between further labour immigration and the actual demands for labour.[30] Although generally accepted by the Palestine Administration this principle could not be effective at that time, since the current unemployment rate was much higher than the approved Pool of 1,000 unemployed.[31]

Since the Zionist demand for a large pool had in practice been turned down, the Executive, having been asked to present its estimate for the First Schedule (July-September 1922), submitted a list of 2,400 skilled and unskilled 'required' workers, mainly for building (1,650) and agricultural (500) projects.[32] But the Administration, disregarding the Zionist estimate, approved a much smaller Schedule of 425 exclusively skilled labourers. At the same time the Executive was warned that any failure on the part of the Zionist Offices to introduce genuinely skilled persons or to obtain immediate employment for them upon arrival, would lead to the abolition of the entire system.[33] From the Zionist point of view, the outcome of the First Schedule was more than disappointing. Of the 425 issued certificates only 180 were used during the approved quarter. Subsequent to further Zionist demands, the Administration agreed to prolong the validity of the unused certificates for an additional period, but even this did not prevent the loss of about one third of them.[34]

Before these unsatisfactory results became known the Administration had issued a much larger Schedule of 1,050 certificates for the successive quarter (October-December 1922). This was due to a significant improvement in economic activities during the summer, which had caused the unemployment rate to drop to 1,600 and the Government's decision to enlarge the Pool to 1,500 unemployed. Following this decision 400 unskilled workers were included in the new Schedule.[35] The outcome of the second Schedule however, was even worse than the first, since this time less than one half of the Zionist candidates turned up during the approved period.[36]

The failure of the Schedule system during the first stages of its operation was due to various factors, most of which were beyond Zionist control. First were the principles of the system itself. According to these principles, the Schedule had to be classified under three headings: particular trade, specific employers and countries of origin. Certain candidates had also to be indicated by name.[37] These terms made the system necessarily very rigid, complicated and unworkable in practice. As far as local employers were concerned, it seems that the Palestine Executive did not meet with many difficulties in obtaining 'vacancies' with specific employers, despite the existing high rate of unemployment. However, most of these enterprises were in the building branch and the trades required (masons, moulders, stone cutters, carpenters and joiners) were not too common among Jews of Eastern Europe. This made the task of the Palestine Offices in finding qualified persons of these trades among their candidates for immigration very difficult, if not impossible.[38]

No less considerable was the notoriety of the economic situation in Palestine. News of the unemployment crisis, the return of many immigrants who had failed to settle down, the stories about the 'most rigid' examinations conducted by the immigration officials in Palestine and finally the deportation of many irregular cases, had apparently had a very significant effect on the general desire to immigrate to Palestine.[39] Hence, the real problem of the Zionists in those days was not, in fact, how to obtain larger Schedules, but rather how best to utilize them.

It seems that the failure of the Zionist Offices to obtain suitable immigrants as stated by the Schedule compelled them to fill their quotas with available candidates who were not in every case qualified as required. This might explain the large number of irregularities within the Schedule, which appeared in various forms: boys were sent as skilled artisans, sisters as wives or even as mothers; some immigrants, when questioned by the immigration officials refused to recognise their own 'names' or those of relatives appearing on their passports, while others gave different trades than those for which they had been scheduled.[40]

The misuse of the Scheduled system, and the various problems which it raised, strengthened the demand of the Palestine Executive for abolishing the existing system and replacing it by the Labour Pool. A scheme based on the principles of the Pool would enable the Palestine Offices to introduce almost all their candidates for immigration, irrespective of the qualifications required by the Schedule.[41] Moreover, deportations of irregular cases on grounds of skill or age would not occur. Nevertheless, certain that Samuel would insist on the continuation of the Schedule system and at the same time accepting the Zionist Executive's policy which was presented to them personally by Dr. Weizmann, the Palestine Executive was eventually compelled to accept the Schedule. However, they did so only on condition that they might be allowed a fixed 'minimum number of certificates' — perhaps 1,500 quarterly.[42]

The Zionist Executive, however, while negotiating with the Colonial Office over the final draft of the revised scheme, presented more concrete and constructive proposals. These proposals were primarily concerned with the Zionist short-comings in control over the Schedule as experience had shown. In order to adjust the scheme to the actual ability of the Organisation to control the Schedule in the optimal way, the Executive suggested various technical amendments:

a) to prolong the period of the Schedule to cover one year;
b) likewise, to prolong the required period for preparation of the Schedule from six weeks to three months;
c) to authorise the Zionist Organisation to apportion and allocate the certificates among the Palestine Offices;
d) to abolish the cross-division of the Schedule under trades and countries of origin.[43]

The Zionist diplomatic campaign in London and Jerusalem to simplify the schedule system and enlarge their powers of control over labour immigration, was accompanied by the introduction of more adequate measures for tightening central control over the Palestine Offices. These measures were primarily concerned with the necessity to convince the British of their ability to control the Offices' activities more effectively and to put an end to all irregularities and short-comings.[44] Following the British-Zionist agreement in February 1923, the Zionist Executive promised to send an inspector to the Offices to explain the principles of the new immigration scheme. However, the main task of Dennis Cohen, a former official of the Department of Immigration and Travel, who was chosen for that mission, was to examine and improve on the spot methods of selection and introduction of immigrants within the Schedule.[45] At the same time, the Executive insisted on regaining authority from the Palestine Executive for allocating the Schedule, in order to obtain direct control over the work of the Palestine Offices.

The Palestine Executive did not agree to Cohen's mission,[46] or to surrender any of its powers of control to the Zionist Executive in London.[47] Although they were also aware of the eventual hampering effects of irregularities on their relations with the Government,[48] their first concern was the impact of the existing economic situation in Palestine on the general volume of immigration. In other words, they sought to reduce the undesirable effects of the unemployment crisis, deportations and the increasing rate of emigration from the country, on the extent of the Schedule and its successful execution.[49] Since the Schedule was determined according to the rate of unemployment, the chief indicator of which was the number of idle immigrants in the Zionist Immigration Camps, the Executive was at constant pains to evacuate the Camps as soon as possible.[50] An additional reason for speedy evacuation of the Camps was the financial distress of the Executive, which made it impossible for them to maintain a large number of immigrants for a long time.[51] The very limited means of the Executive also prevented it from settling many newcomers in agricultural settlements subsidised by the Organisation. A cheaper and easier short term alternative was to send the new arrivals to friends and relatives in the country. To this end, the Palestine Executive urged the Palestine Offices to assist them by giving first priority in their selection to immigrants with a certain amount of independent means, or with relatives in Palestine who were in a position to support them.[52]

By recommending that immigrants be included in the limited Schedule, when they might otherwise have applied for visas under one of the unlimited categories, the Executive was indirectly suggesting a reduction in the general volume of immigration. The Executive did not stop, however, at mere recommendations, but sent the largest Office in Warsaw a list of candidates with relatives in Palestine to whom the Office was asked to give priority within its quota. Despite strong protests by the Warsaw Office against what they considered an 'unbearable intervention in their powers of discretion',[53] the Palestine Executive continued to warn and urge all Palestine Offices to be 'strict' and 'cautious' and to select exclusively people who would be able to settle down in Palestine without any financial help from the Executive.[54] Furthermore, following frequent complaints from 'exasperated' immigrants, the Executive instructed the Offices to make it clear to all immigrants coming under the Schedule that the Organisation would not accept any responsibility for their economic absorption in Palestine.[55] This approach seemed unavoidable, although it vigorously contradicted the principle of the 'guarantee system' which the Zionists were so anxious to restore. However, considering the existing circumstances and since Samuel himself disregarded any guarantees on the part of the Zionist Organisation (preferring to determine the Schedule solely according to actual labour requirements), the responsibility of the Executive over these immigrants could rightly have been considered as moral rather than material.

But attempts by the Palestine Executive to avoid actual responsibility for immigrants coming under the Schedule did not release them from being held morally responsible for their employment. This was particularly emphasised by the 'somewhat alarming' total Jewish emigration of 1,443 during June-August 1923. The fact that 1,059 of the emigrants were newcomers and only 374 were old residents,[56] signified the failure of the Palestine Executive to absorb labour immigration.

These circumstances caused the Colonial Office, at the end of September 1923, to consider favourably Hyamson's proposal suggesting temporary suspension of labour immigration.[57] However, strong Zionist reaction left no doubt concerning the grave political effect of such a move. Joseph Cowen, of the Zionist Executive, who was called to the Colonial Office in Weizmann's absence from London, pointed out the 'most unfortunate' political implications of any official stoppage and suggested that 'if immigration is to be restricted the Zionist Organisation should take the initiative and limit themselves to the figures that the Colonial Office think desirable.'[58] Nevertheless, since the current Schedule for the last quarter of 1923 was fixed at 100 certificates only, the Zionist Executive felt that if a more liberal Schedule could not be obtained 'the Zionist Organisation would be in a stronger position if it was able to deny that immigration had been suspended or a nominal Schedule fixed and state in general terms that certificates were available and would be distributed by the Organisation in strict accordance with the economic situation in Palestine'.[59]

This 'no war, no peace' policy found considerable 'understanding' at the Colonial Office. Sydney Moody, who discussed the matter on behalf of the Colonial Office, agreed that for the time being no definite Schedule should be fixed and visas under category 'E' should be granted 'in such numbers as the state of the labour market might warrant'. It was accordingly recognised that this arrangement 'implies in effect that the Schedule system is temporarily suspended'.[60] However, this 'gentleman's agreement' was not eventually approved by the Colonial Office or by the Zionist Executive. Shuckburgh insisted that 'drastic restrictions are required'[61] and informed the Zionist Executive that the Schedule should be limited to the nominal figure of 100, as approved by the Palestine Government. At the same time Cowen, recommending the 'agreement' before the Zionist Executive, placed himself in the minority. Despite Dr. Ruppin's depressing report to the Executive regarding the unemployment crisis in Palestine and his predictions of 3,000-4,000 unemployed in November 'unless immediate steps were taken',[62] the Executive adopted a resolution to support the Palestine Executive's request for a Schedule of 500 (certificates). It was further suggested that Cowen would meet Shuckburgh and offer him a new 'agreement', in which the Schedule should be nominally fixed at 500, but it 'being understood that the most sparing use would be made of the certificates'.[63]

At that very time, the Palestine Executive was confronted with the same dilemma. But since the Administration had meanwhile agreed to extend the period of the Schedule to six months, as had been requested by the Zionists themselves, the actual dilemma of the Executive was whether to ask for 500 certificates for that period or the same figure for the next quarter only.[64] Professor Pick, recommending that the six month Schedule be accepted, pointed out the possible advantage of long-term planning which would enable the Executive to introduce more flexibility in allocation of the certificates and allow sufficient time to the Palestine Offices for 'training' and selecting the most desirable elements for Palestine. However, as on many previous occasions, the political considerations again overcame the practical, causing the Executive to adopt Sprinzak's point of view in favour of 500 certificates for the current quarter, thus allowing the Executive to ask for further certificates for the following quarter.[65]

The rather unexpected, but nevertheless very significant improvement in the economic situation from the spring of 1924 onwards, increased the need for labour in the country and consequently the Administration was more ready to enlarge the Schedule accordingly.[66] These circumstances placed the Palestine Executive in an unprecedented dilemma: whether to utilize all the issued certificates at once or to act more cautiously and despatch them to the Palestine Offices by instalments.[67] Sprinzak, pressing for a more daring policy, advocated immediate use of the whole Schedule and even an attempt to secure a supplementary one. Moreover, pointing out the recent enormous response to immigration in Eastern Europe and the unlimited demand for labour in the country, he further suggested that the time had come to abolish the Schedule system and allow 'free immigration'. This, he explained, could release the Executive from any moral or material responsibilities for immigrants coming under the Schedule, and would enable the Organisation to use the money at present spent on the operation of the system for more constructive projects, which could create further jobs for immigrants. Colonel Kisch, although admitting that the Zionists' 'ultimate aim' should be to secure the recognition of the principle that 'every Jew had a natural right to come to Palestine', could not favour the idea of lifting control over immigration entirely. As far as he was concerned it would be 'fatal' to allow anything like 'free immigration' particularly during the early stages of the building up of the National Home when immigration 'must be selected so as to ensure the maximum and most productive contribution to the structure'.[68]

Since the Executive apparently anticipated that the Administration would not finally approve their complete demands, they preferred to inflate them in order to secure a better bargaining stand. These calculations, however, more than once placed the Executive in a delicate position when the Administration approved a larger Schedule than they had originally expected. In the spring of 1925, for example, the Executive asked for 10,000 certificates for the bi-annual Schedule starting in April. The Administration approved a Schedule of 6,000 — more, it seems, than the Zionists had expected. The Treasurer, van Vriesland, brought to the attention of his colleagues the financial difficulties of the Executive, which would prevent proper absorption of large numbers of immigrants at once, and recommended the allotment of the certificates by instalments. Furthermore, contradicting the 'optimistic' predictions regarding the future demand for labour, van Vriesland insisted that the Executive itself should reduce the Schedule by suspending part of the certificates already approved. In his view, 'immigration should be regulated according to the economic demands of the country and not upon the demand for immigration abroad'. Kisch, however, rejected the idea of suspending part of the certificates, as he feared this might lead to the Government's loss of confidence in the reliability of future Zionist estimates, particularly since their original demand had already been drastically reduced. Instead, he suggested despatching the whole Schedule at once, while instructing the Palestine Offices to allocate their quotas strictly by instalments.[69]

The apparent evasion of its well-recognised powers to

regulate labour immigration, by relying on the Palestine Offices on this matter, brought the Palestine Executive to a very critical position by the end of 1925. During the last four months of 1925 an unprecedented record of 5,600 labourers (apart from their families) entered the country, raising the number of unemployed to 3,000. Yet, since the Executive did not realise the severity of the situation and failed to anticipate the impending economic crisis, they refused to adopt any precautionary measures, such as temporary suspension or regulation of the flow of additional labour into the country. Despite the fact that a further 10,000 immigrants were already expected for the first quarter of 1926, the Executive persisted in its radical policy. In the absence of Dr. Ruppin and van Vriesland, the more moderate members of the Executive, Kisch often placed himself in the minority by advocating a more realistic and moderate policy. Professor Pick and Sprinzak, the two other members, who remained Directors of Immigration and Labour respectively, constantly pressed for an enlargement of the Schedule and for securing supplementary and advance quotas against the Schedules to come, in order to supply the need of the Palestine Offices for more certificates. As far as they were concerned, the existing crisis which they believed would soon most likely disappear, should by no means affect the Executive's policy. Anxious to avoid discouragement of immigration by revealing their difficulties, they emphasised the importance of obtaining large Schedules.[70]

Nevertheless, Pick and Sprinzak disagreed over the instructions to be sent to the Palestine Offices. Pick, concerned about the expense of maintaining the immigrants in Immigration Camps, suggested instructing the Offices to select only those with relatives in Palestine who would be able to support them. Sprinzak, on the other hand, pointed out that in fact most of those 'relatives' did not take care of their 'dependants' anyhow, and insisted that the Offices should give first priority to real pioneers whose 'Zionist consciousness' and 'physical fitness' were undisputed. Accordingly, the Executive rejected Kisch's proposal in favour of 1,200 for the first quarter of 1926 and recommended a larger one of 3,000 to consist of 700 'dependent' immigrants, 300 pioneers and 2,000 selected according to the discretion of the Palestine Offices.[71]

The Government's definite rejection of the Zionists' demands and the remarkable increase in unemployment which reached 5,000-6,000 during the winter, eventually compelled the Palestine Executive to adopt Kisch's point of view and to reduce their original demand to 500 immigrants only.[72] No less considerable was the increasing rate of emigration from Palestine during the first half of 1926 which reached an unprecedented record of 980 emigrants in June only.[73] Nevertheless, it took the Executive almost a year from the first signs of the new crisis to admit the severity of the situation, and agree to adopt drastic measures.

At the end of August 1926, when the distribution of a new Schedule was on the agenda, the Palestine Executive finally reached a unanimous resolution in favour of immediate enforcement of all the precautionary measures which they had hitherto hesitated to adopt, namely:

a) temporary suspension of half of the 2,500 certificates approved for the current Schedule by the Executive itself until a significant improvement in the economic situation could be seen;

b) suspension of the allotted certificates by the Palestine Offices until further instructions from the Palestine Executive;

c) to inform directly from Jerusalem all candidates for immigration of the truth about the economic conditions in Palestine;

d) to instruct the Palestine Offices to introduce most strict selection criteria regarding the candidates' Zionist consciousness, their genuine dependence on relatives in Palestine and possession of sufficient means for maintenance during their first months in Palestine.[74]

The drastic measures adopted by the Palestine Executive after such delay were very unlikely to restrain the swiftly increasing unemployment rate, or to ease the great flow of emigration from the country. Nevertheless, although the volume of labour immigration from September 1926 onwards dropped very significantly, this could not be exclusively attributed to the Government's restrictions on the Schedule, or to the new course endorsed by the Palestine Executive. The natural impulse for migration which derives from the obvious desire to improve one's livelihood was taking its toll, as a result of the economic crisis in Palestine. As a matter of fact, a remarkable decline in labour immigration had already begun in January 1926, a long time before the new restrictions were actually introduced. Furthermore, only 4,000 out of the 10,000 immigrants expected to arrive during the first quarter of 1926 eventually entered the country.

Most of these candidates, already furnished with immigration certificates, apparently changed their minds and postponed their departure. This might be attributed chiefly to the discouraging reports coming from Palestine and the thousands who returned to their countries of origin, bearing dreadful stories about the country.[75]

In the light of these consequences it would not be inaccurate to conclude that the economic conditions in Palestine had a far more substantial effect on the general desire to immigrate to Palestine than had the actual British or Zionist policies. Moreover, it seems obvious that the principle of Economic Absorptive Capacity found its most reliable interpretation in the natural mechanism of immigration which official policy and political considerations could not entirely distort.

IMMIGRATION UNDER CATEGORY 'D':
THE CASE OF THE FIANCÉES

Since the Labour Schedule was limited numerically and consisted mostly of skilled labour, the Palestine Offices faced serious difficulties in securing visas for all their candidates for immigration. Under these circumstances the Offices were compelled to seek other alternatives to obtain visas for those people. One such alternative was to 'enlarge' families of immigrants by attaching to them 'relatives' who had failed to obtain a visa.[76] A second option which apparently proved more practical, was to claim 'dependence' on residents of Palestine under category 'D'.[77] These tactics might to a large extent explain the numerous irregularities, particularly during the new scheme's first year of operation.[78]

Once the Administration realised that a large number of these 'dependants' were in fact workers who eventually entered the labour market, aggravating the country's unemployment,[79] policy regarding category 'D' became, in many aspects, identical to that of category 'E'. Immigrants coming under both categories had to possess immigration certificates for dependants were also suspended.[81] Likewise, immigration was temporarily suspended in March 1922, certificates for dependents were also suspended.[81] Likewise, when it was decided in May 1922 to resume labour immigration, this time according to Schedules, the ban on dependants was lifted accordingly.[82] Nevertheless, considering that immigration under category 'D' was not limited numerically, in times when restrictions on the Schedule were imposed, many legitimate candidates for the Schedule apparently used Category 'D' as a substitute.[83] For this reason the Palestine Government, while considering the inauguration of the Labour Schedules, suggested regulating the immigration of dependants more adequately by including them in the Schedule.[84]

This proposition eventually did not materialise, at any rate not during the years of economic depression, when the Schedules were mostly devoted to skilled labour. Therefore the Palestine Offices were forced, in some cases, to 'adjust' the qualifications of their candidates to the requirements of the Schedule.[85] However, it was almost impossible to persuade the British Consuls that young females were genuinely skilled workers, trained in various branches of building, industry or agriculture. At the same time the Zionists could not remain indifferent to the indirect restrictions on immigration of women, whose presence in Palestine was described as 'vital' from both social and economic points of view. The Palestine Executive, when pressing for the constitution of the Labour Pool, had indicated that the Pool could solve this question entirely.[86] On the other hand, the Zionist Executive, while negotiating the final draft of the new immigration scheme in London, eventually succeeded in securing the Colonial Office's permission for fiancées of residents of Palestine to be allowed to obtain visas under Category 'D'.[87] The immediate results of the enforcement of this provision were very significant, considering the steep rise in immigration of women during the second quarter of 1923, and the fact that single girls constituted over 75 per cent of the total figure.[88]

The method for obtaining certificates for fiancées appeared to be rather simple and at the same time it was almost impossible to prove it had been done with the deliberate intention of evading the law. Originally, if the applicant could prove that he was in a position to maintain a wife, his word and that of his guarantors were accepted and his application approved. Whether or not the applicant later married his fiancée was a difficult and costly matter to follow up. However, in cases where after a reasonable interval enquiries revealed that marriage had not taken place, the Administration stood helpless in the face of the reply that 'the couple had changed their minds'.[89]

Albert Hyamson, then Controller of Labour, was convinced that unfair advantage had been taken of that humanitarian provision and that at least 75 per cent of the applications concerned had been made in bad faith. As far as he was concerned, 'much of the unemployment among Jewish women had to be attributed to the success of those fraudulent applications'.[90] However, he was unable to take any direct action on that question until November 1923 when he became Acting Director of the Immigration Department and subsequently Controller of Permits. His first undertaking in that direction was to consult the Attorney General regarding legal and administrative measures 'which might put an end to that abuse'.[91]

As regards legal measures to be adopted Norman Bentwich drew Hyamson's attention to relevant articles of the existing law, in which proceedings could be brought against both the eligible applicant and his 'fiancée' on charges of false pretences and statements.[92] Such action, however, could not be very effective because of its deterrent rather than prohibitory nature. Moreover, the subsequent legal proceedings and possible deportations from the country were likely to lead to heavy expenses and undesirable political friction in the case of deportation.[93] Regarding administrative measures, the Attorney General suggested that applicants should be required to produce a contract of engagement (to marry) as a necessary document to obtain a certificate for a fiancée.[94] The last proposal was eventually adopted,[95] but apparently failed to bring about any satisfactory results. Although Hyamson had no doubts that the Zionist Organisation and particularly the Office in Warsaw were not only encouraging, but even organising that 'fraudulent practice whenever possible', he could do no more than instruct the British authorities concerned to exercise stricter examination and if necessary, investigation in each case.[96]

A radical, although temporary solution to this unpleasant question, was found in July 1925. Since most of the girls coming under category 'D' belonged to the working class, they entered the labour market whether they got married or not, so that the question of their being a genuine or false fiancée consequently became irrelevant. As category 'E' was intended to include all persons who found employment in Palestine it therefore seemed proper to admit these girls not under category 'D' but category 'E'.[97] Accordingly, the Administration came to the conclusion that a provision in category 'D' should be made, in which 'Jewish women who belonged to the working or the lower middle class and were between the ages of 18 and 35 and able bodied', had to be included in the Labour Schedule. However, women who answered these requirements only in part or not at all continued to be eligible for immigration under category 'D' according to the previous procedure. The Zionists acquiesced in this provision.[98]

The difficulties concerning admission of fiancées were thus removed, although not for long. During the economic crisis of 1927-28, when the Schedules were severely restricted and eventually suspended, immigration of all Jewish girls, whether they were genuinely fiancées or merely dependent on Palestine residents, was temporarily postponed.[99] Thus, the Zionists' acquiescence in the above-mentioned provision might retrospectively be considered to have been erroneous.[100]

At any rate, the lack of reaction on the part of the Palestine Executive to the new method of admitting women was undoubtedly attributable to the fact that at the time the

Labour Schedules were larger than ever before and consisted of vast numbers of females.[101] These circumstances apparently enabled the Palestine Offices to introduce most of the women pioneers within the Schedule. Furthermore, irregularities under category 'D' were likely to be reduced. Where mass immigration was concerned, the Palestine Executive was interested more than ever in consolidating its control over labour immigration and in preventing the unselective flow of so-called fiancées.[102]

From the Zionist point of view, the advantages of these arrangements were even more significant during the economic crisis. The new method enabled the Palestine Executive to restrict the immigration of women more adequately by reducing their ration in the Schedule and using their certificates for introducing men.[103] These measures were indispensable, considering the grave unemployment among women workers, many of whom were suffering the distress of hunger.[104] Nevertheless, the Palestine Executive never openly admitted that they regarded this unwritten arrangement favourably.

Finally, it is worthwhile pointing out that the Zionist policy regarding category 'D' as a whole was to a large extent ambiguous and inconsistent. This attitude derived mainly from lack of social and economic uniformity within this class. The two main relevant qualifications were: a) the extent of dependence on the Palestine residents, and b) the degree of productivity of the dependant himself.

During the economic depression when labour immigration was restricted and the Schedules consisted mainly of skilled labour, the Palestine Executive was in a dilemma regarding immigration under category 'D'. The fundamental question was whether to encourage unlimited immigration of 'dependants' under this category, or to include them in the Labour Schedule, which meant restricting their numbers. Eventually, the latter policy was adopted and the Palestine Offices were instructed to give priority to 'dependants' in the Schedule, even at the expense of their relative lack of productivity and Zionist consciousness.[105] During the economic boom, the Executive did not interfere much with the Offices' control over dependants. However, towards the end of 1925 when an economic crisis became apparent, the Executive brought back its previous policy in stricter form by recommending the issue of special certificates for the exclusive use of 'dependants' coming under the Labour Schedule.[106]

MIDDLE CLASS IMMIGRATION

One must realise that Palestine during the period concerned was only one among many other destinations to which Jews could have migrated and from several points of view not the most attractive one. When considering economic or personal security, Western Europe and the overseas countries were more likely to offer better conditions than Palestine. To a large extent this might explain the relatively low volume of immigration into Palestine in comparison with other countries and particularly the insignificant numbers belonging to the middle class.[107]

Despite an extremely liberal policy towards immigration during the first year of the Civil Administration less than one fifth of the total Jewish immigration came to Palestine independently, i.e. not under the auspices of the Zionist Organisation.[108] This rate did not change significantly during the three following years when the average number of immigrants under category 'B' reached about 15%. The low percentage of middle class immigrants during this period can be chiefly attributed to the discouraging effects of the economic depression in Palestine, to Arab violence, and to the enforcement of the new immigration policy.

As will be remembered the Colonial Office suggested, and Samuel agreed, that the minimum capital required for immigrants under category 'B' should be £500 or a secure income of £6 per person per month.[109] A comparison of these two qualifications might indicate the considerable amount of capital which was thought to be required to establish an immigrant in industry, agriculture or commercial business. However, in economic and currency terms of Eastern Europe, this figure was apparently unattainable for most of the lower middle class, the likeliest class for immigration.[110]

The Zionist Commission, concerned about the administrative obstacles in the way of this class, urged and eventually succeeded in obtaining, a provision for artisans and craftsmen in possession of at least £120, to be allowed to come under category 'B' provided specific authority of the Immigration Department was given in each case.[111] When negotiations on the new scheme were taking place in London at the end of 1921, the Zionist Executive suggested, and the Colonial Office agreed, to legitimise this provisional arrangement by creating a new category 'H'. This category had to consist of persons who, while not strictly speaking of independent means were nevertheless likely to be able to make a living for themselves, either as retail shopkeepers or as craftsmen working on their own. However, Samuel, out of his concern about unemployment in the country rejected the proposal of creating a new category which might have allowed a flow of destitute immigrants who would eventually enter the labour market. Regarding this class as potential labourers he suggested including them within category 'E'.

Similar, though much stricter, was the policy regarding category 'C', members of learned professions such as physicians, engineers, lawyers etc, who intended to follow their calling in Palestine. In order to restrict immigration of this class and at the same time to prevent entry of artisans and the like, who had also claimed visas under category 'C', the Immigration Department insisted that all applications for this category should also be referred to Jerusalem for approval.[113] In considering these applications the Department intended to take into account the profession of the applicant, the demand for this profession, age, capital, past experience, dependants etc. However, all these qualifications were not distinctly defined, leaving entire control over this category to the exclusive discretion of the Department.[114] Immigration under category 'C' thus became insignificant, constituting less than one per cent of the total volume, until it was finally abolished in November 1924.[115] Subsequently, legitimate immigrants for category 'C' were divided between category 'B' and category 'E' according to the amount of their capital.[116] The logic behind this reclassi-fication was eventually approved by the P.Z.E. itself, which for reasons of its own instructed the Palestine Offices to include artisans, members of professions and persons with limited means within the Labour Schedule.[117] Nevertheless, the Executive insisted that immigrants belonging to these trades who were in possession of £200 should be allowed to enter under category 'B' without being referred to Jerusalem.[118] In the final draft of the immigration scheme which was agreed on between the Colonial Office and the Zionist Executive in February 1923 such a provision was made,[119] but its implementation was officially postponed until the enforcement of the new Ordinance in September 1925.

Meanwhile, the Department of Immigration conducted itself according to its provisional agreement with the Zionist Commission (of September 1921) and was ready to consider favourably immigrants of independent means, even if their capital was limited to £50 only, provided special authority from Jerusalem was given for each case.[120] This policy was endorsed by the Director of Commerce and Industry who offered the assistance of his Department for the satisfactory economic absorption of such immigrants.[121]

Nevertheless, despite the liberal policy regarding immigrants of independent means, neither their numbers nor their aggregate capital could be considered significant. Immigrants with substantial capital refrained from coming, apparently because of the economic depression.[122] At the same time, with the lack of adequate public and Zionist resources or import of private capital, any radical improvement in the economic situation was unlikely.

This obstacle was finally removed in summer 1924 by an unanticipated flow of middle class immigration. During the following 18 months (from June 1924 to November 1925) an unprecedented 16,000 immigrants entered the country under category 'B', in possession of an average capital of about £600 per family.[123] However, this remarkable influx of middle class immigration could by no means be attributed to the incentive policy of the Government regarding this class, but rather to external factors. As a result of radical monetary and fiscal reforms in Poland at the beginning of 1924, the economic position of the local middle class, which consisted mostly of Jews, was severely affected. In the same year, entry to the United States, particularly for immigrants from

Eastern Europe, became almost impossible, following new restrictions on immigration. The incidental combination of these two factors made Palestine, for the first time, the major country in the world for Jewish immigration. In the course of two years 55,000 immigrants entered the country, almost doubling the figure of the existing Jewish population.

The greater part of the new arrivals, particularly those belonging to the middle class, turned to Tel Aviv, the new Jewish town near Jaffa, whose population was subsequently increased from 21,000 in June 1924 to 40,000 at the end of 1925. This extraordinarily rapid growth during such a short period had an immense effect on the density of living accommodation in the town and consequently on the demand for housing, plots, building materials and on their respective prices. In response to this demand and the very promising profits in the building industry, economic activity in the town concentrated around this industry. Three quarters of the total investment in 1925 (about £1.5 million) was devoted to building, and many other industries were designed to meet the immediate needs of this branch.[124] Everything appeared to depend upon the continuous influx of middle class immigration, bringing capital with them, building a house and then apparently waiting for the next lot of immigrants with capital to provide them with a living. At the same time, the constant flow of money into the market caused a sharp increase in prices and correspondingly raised the cost of living.[125]

The Palestine Government, seriously concerned about this, regarded the abnormal development of Tel Aviv as an unhealthy and risky phenomenon which was likely to lead, sooner or later, to an unavoidable crash, unless some 'really productive' industries were established in the town.[126] Hyamson however, was of the opinion that an immediate remedy for such a disaster might be found in new restrictions on middle class immigration. As far as he was concerned, immigrants with £500 and less led to an undue proportion of 'non-productive elements' which took to peddling, shop-keeping, land speculation and moneylending and were almost 'at the end of their tether'. In view of their ages, training and mentality he was convinced that most of them were unsuited for manual labour if such were available.[127] Anxious about the type of middle class immigration and the recent reports from Eastern Europe suggesting that about a million Jews (!) were intending to come in the near future,[128] he advocated urgent restrictions on immigration of persons of independent means. In practical terms this meant excluding people who had only between £500 to £1,000 by raising the minimum qualification to the latter figure.[129]

The news of Hyamson's new plan, and of his apparent success in persuading Samuel and John Shuckburgh of the necessity to restrict middle class immigration, caused anger and anxiety among Zionist circles in London.[130] Weizmann regarded Hyamson's proposal as 'dangerous' and 'preposterous' and made a strong representation to the Colonial Office in an attempt to revoke it. The Secretary of State, on the advice of Shuckburgh, asked Weizmann to approve a Committee of Enquiry to go to Palestine to study the question of Tel Aviv and immigration in general. This was also rejected by Weizmann, who undertook to furnish the Colonial Office with a memorandum setting out the views and proposals of the Zionist Executive on this matter.[131] The Zionists thus succeeded in evading any immediate amendments of the Regulation and securing the Colonial Office's assurance that such changes 'will not be imposed without further consultations with them'.[132] When the promised memo was eventually submitted to the Colonial Office, after a delay of seven months,[133] the proposed amendments had already lost their acuteness following the developments which took place in Palestine.

While these negotiations were taking place in London, Hyamson did not abandon the subject, examining all possible ways of tightening control over immigration of this class. As far as amendments of the Regulations were concerned, it seems that he could not have chosen a more inconvenient time for his campaign than the summer of 1925. Samuel, whose term of office in Palestine was coming to an end, leaving in its wake unprecedented prosperity, was very unlikely to recommend such controversial restrictions on the eve of his departure. However, it was not inconceivable that his successor, Lord Plumer, would impose them during his first days in office. Nevertheless, in the middle of September, the new High Commissioner summoned a conference on immigration questions in the presence of the Chief Secretary, the Attorney General and the Controller of Permits and also invited Colonel Kisch to represent the views of the Palestine Zionist Executive. Hyamson took this opportunity of recommending the raising of capital qualifications for immigrants of independent means to £1,000 or even £1,500 and immigrants with smaller amounts would be left to the discretion of the Permit Section. Likewise, agricultural settlers would be limited numerically according to the resources of the Palestine Zionist Executive and 'other responsible bodies'. Kisch, emphasising the large amount of the aggregate capital which was being brought by these immigrants and the extent to which the development of the country was dependent on their resources, strongly deprecated Hyamson's proposals. As far as Kisch was concerned, middle class immigration would, when necessary, restrict itself 'through the normal intervention of economic laws' and thus any arbitrary restrictions would be superfluous. The High Commissioner, although expressing himself rather strongly with regard to the excessive proportion of immigrants with small means, avoided an immediate resolution of this matter.[134]

The proposed amendment of the Regulations regarding immigrants of independent means soon lost its acute importance, following the enforcement of the new Immigration Ordinance in September 1925. The direct cause of this was Article 4 (1) of the new Regulations which stated that no immigrant would be allowed to enter Palestine unless he possessed an Immigration Certificate granted by the Chief Immigration Officer. Accordingly, all applicants for visas to Palestine, without exception, had to be referred to Jerusalem for approval. The effect of this procedure on immigration in general and particularly on persons of independent means was immediate and very substantial. Their volume dropped drastically during the last quarter of 1925 to 1,414 immigrants, in comparison with 3,314 under this category in the previous quarter (a reduction of over 60 per cent), and to a monthly average of less than 200 during the first six months of 1926. The total immigration of persons of independent means in 1926 consisted only of 13 per cent of the corresponding volume of the previous year, 1,325 as compared with 10,127 respectively. In view of these small returns, amendment of the Regulation regarding immigration of independent means was superfluous. Yet Hyamson was still of the opinion that the qualification of immigrants under new Category 'A' should be increased from £500 to £1,000 and of 'B' from £250 to £500 and that a provision should be added to the latter stating that 'subject to the discretion of the Chief Immigration Officer, whose discretion will be guided by, inter alia, the previous occupation of the prospective immigrant, his prospective occupation, his apparent suitability for it and his prospects of success therein in view of his means and experience'.[135]

Although Hyamson's proposals were not officially enforced until May 1926 following revised Instructions to the Consuls, his system had been operative from September 1925 in consequence of the implementation of Article 4(1). The reference of all applications to Jerusalem could enable the Permit Section to decide upon the merits of each case concerning the issue of an Immigration Certificate. Moreover, in view of the enormous additional work which this procedure involved and the very limited staff of the Section, delays of two to three months were almost unavoidable.[136]

The Zionists, alarmed by the fact that since the enforcement of the new Ordinance not a single visa had been granted, and anticipating delays which the new procedure might involve, had already stirred themselves into action at the beginning of October. Weizmann called at the Colonial Office again and made 'very serious representations' to the Secretary of State. Referring to the deteriorating economic situation in Poland which was rapidly devaluing the financial means of the local middle class, he described the procrastination in granting Certificates as 'tantamount to stopping the immigration' of this class. He asked for the intervention of the Colonial Office in shortening the procedure to a reasonable time such as a fortnight at the most.[137]

Simultaneously, Kisch made 'sharp representations' to the

High Commissioner and to Symes, the new Chief Secretary. At his meeting with Symes, Kisch pointed out that the failure of the Permit Section to dispose of Certificates for persons of independent means was keeping not less than £100,000 a month out of the country.[138] This argument seems to have convinced Symes, who granted all the additional staff for which Hyamson had been fighting, and within two or three days all the outstanding applications from immigrants of independent means had been disposed of.[139]

Nevertheless, the implementation of the controversial Article 4(1) and the inevitable delays which it involved continued to occupy both the Government and the Zionists throughout 1926 and eventually brought about fresh reorganisation of the immigration machinery[140] and revised Regulations. However, the actual effect of these issues on the extent of middle class immigration gradually diminished, following the economic crisis in both Poland and Palestine. Kisch's indication, at the Immigration Conference mentioned above, that middle class immigration would, when necessary, restrict itself through the normal intervention of economic laws, materialised sooner and far more substantially than was anticipated at that moment. In fact, the decrease in immigrants of independent means had already begun in July 1925, two months before the enforcement of the new Ordinance.[141] Although this tendency was very significantly accelerated by the implementation of the Ordinance its continuation was undoubtedly inevitable because of the economic factors.

The turning point in Poland came during the middle of 1925, when the value of the zloty against foreign currencies began to fall rapidly.[142] A middle class applicant who had reasonable hope of producing £500 at the time of his application might not be able to produce this sum two or three months later, when his application was finally approved.[143] This might explain the vigorous Zionist campaign to shorten the procedure concerned, but nevertheless could hardly justify their complaint that this procedure was the dominant cause of the sudden drop in middle class immigration.

In addition to the effects of the economic crisis in Poland the reports from Palestine towards the end of 1925 might have had an even more discouraging influence. Most of the applicants of this class who were eventually supplied with Certificates had ceased to show any interest in them,[144] presumably preferring the devil they knew to the one they did not. In view of these circumstances, fresh Zionist initiative focusing itself on the demand for authorising the Immigration Officer in Warsaw to dispose of applications for visas under the independent means category without reference to Jerusalem,[145] was very unlikely to bring about any radical change in the situation.

NOTES

[1] Cmd. 1700, June 1922, p. 19.

[2] Shuckburgh, minutes dated 20.6.22, C.O.733/36 file 29270.

[3] Samuel's statement at Government House, 3.6.21, enclosed in his despatch 139 to Churchill, 6.6.21, C.O.733/3 file 30263. See also Chapter 3 above pp. 38-9.

[4] See Chapter 5 pp. 84-6.

[5] For a comprehensive review of these questions see 'Memorandum on the Control of Immigration to Palestine 1920-1930', 16.7.30, I.S.A. 11/40/2.

[6] F.O. to H.M. Representatives abroad, circulars 50 and 51, 15.6.21, F.O. 371/6383 file E6724/144/88.

[7] For example see correspondence in C.O.733/10 file 32925.

[8] Clauson, minutes dated 8.7.21, ibid.

[9] Z.O. Central Office, London, to Z.C. Jerusalem, 6.11.21, C.Z.A. S6/269.

[10] See 'Public Notice, Admission of Immigration into Palestine, 1.8.21', in Official Gazette No. 49, 15.8.21. See Appendix 3.

[11] Samuel to Churchill, tel. 502, 14.12.21, C.O.733/8 file 62256.

[12] Z.C. Jerusalem to Palestine (Zionist) Offices in circulars regarding immigration, 6.9.21, 20.9.21, C.Z.A., S6/267.

[13] Samuel to Churchill, tel. 360, 5.9.21, C.O.733/6 file 44737; Samuel to Churchill tel. 381, 21.9.21, C.O.733/6 file 47443.

[14] See note 12 above.

[15] P.Z.E. to Palestine Offices, Circular Letter, 25.12.21, C.Z.A., S6/267.

[16] P.Z.E., Labour Department in circular to Labour Departments of Palestine Offices, February 1922, C.Z.A., S6/267.

[17] W. Deedes, for the H.C., to Churchill, confidential despatch, 10.3.22, C.O.733/19 file 13565. The Z.E. had already admitted in January that 'the actual number of unemployed workmen in Palestine is about 2,000', but it instructed the Palestine Offices that 'for many reasons this number ought, at the present moment, not to be made public', Circular, January 1922, C.Z.A., Z4/3075. See also P.Z.E. Minutes of Meeting 10.1.22, C.Z.A. unclassified.

[18] See Chapter 4 above, p. 69.

[19] Samuel to Churchill, tel. 91, 9.3.22, C.O.733/19 file 11623.

[20] Ibid, ibid.

[21] C.O. to F.O., 15.3.22, ibid; F.O. circular to H.M. Consuls, 8.4.22, F.O. 372/1916 file T3303/147/388.

[22] Shuckburgh, minute dated 11.3.22, C.O.733/19 file 11623; see also Chapter 3 above, p. 57.

[23] Total immigration during March-May — 2,216; June-August — 1,334; see appendix 6.

[24] 'The Present Position of Immigration into Palestine', memo by S. Finkelstein, C.Z.A., London, 9.11.22, C.Z.A. L3/31.

[25] Official Gazette, April-September 1922.

[26] See Chapter 6, pp. 95-6.

[27] Wyndham Deedes, Acting H.C. to Churchill, tel. 521, 30.12.21, C.O.733/8 file 245.

[28] Deedes to Churchill, confidential despatch, 10.3.22, C.O.733/19 file 13565; C.O. to Z.O., 28.3.22, F.O. 372/1916 file T3858/147/388; Deedes to Weizmann, personal, 30.3.22, C.Z.A., Z4/16145; Shuckburgh to Weizmann, private, March 1922, Z4/16146.

[29] L. Stein to C.O., 10.3.22, C.O.733/36 file 11723.

[30] See P.Z.E. minutes of meeting, 28.3.22, C.Z.A.; also Chapter 4 above, pp. 69-70.

[31] P.Z.E. minutes of meeting, 10.5.22, C.Z.A.

[32] Kisch to Controller of Labour, 21.4.22, C.Z.A., S6/274.

[33] H. Pick, P.Z.E., Director, Immigration Department, in circular to Palestine Offices, 18.7.22, C.Z.A., S6/267.

[34] Circular to Palestine Offices, 3.1.23, S6/271; Pick to Kisch 7.1.23, ibid; Kisch to Controller of Labour 9.1.23., 28.1.23, both in S6/274.

[35] Hyamson to P.Z.E., 3.11.22, I.S.A. 11/4.

[36] During the last quarter of 1922 only 491 immigrants under category E1 entered the country, apparently part of them only belonging to the preceding Schedule, Kisch to Hyamson, 28.1.23, C.Z.A., S6/274.

[37] See for example Hyamson to P.Z.E., note 35 above.

[38] See report of Joshua Gordon (official of the Zionist Immigration Department, Jerusalem) to the Zionist Executive, London, on his tour to Palestine Offices, minutes of meeting of Z.E., 9.7.24, C.Z.A., Z4/302/11.

[39] See note 24 above.

[40] Kisch to Stein, 22.1.23, C.Z.A., Z4/16085; Imm. Dept., P.Z.E. circulars to the Palestine Offices, 'confidential' 20.5.23, in S6/267; July 1923, ibid; Morris's confidential memorandum regarding irregularities, 12.10.23, C.O.733/50 file 51392; see also 'Memorandum . . . 1920-1930', 16.7.30, note 5 above.

[41] S.A. van Vriesland, P.Z.E. to Chief Secretary, 21.9.22, C.Z.A., L3/31.

[42] See 'Revision of Immigration Regulations', memo by the P.Z.E. submitted to the Palestine Government, 4.12.22, I.S.A. 11/6; also Chapter 6 above pp. 104-5.

[43] See 'Revised Scheme for the Control of Immigration into Palestine' memo by the Z.E., 15.2.23, C.O.733/59 file 8490; minutes of the meeting in C.O. 'to discuss the proposed revised Immigration Regulations . . .', 21.2.23, C.O.733/54 file 9748; also Chapter 6 above, pp. 106-8.

[44] L. Stein to the Under Secretary of State, C.O. 21.9.22, 9.10.22, I.S.A. 2/145.

[45] Stein to Kisch, 15.2.23, C.Z.A., Z4/16085.

[46] Pick to Z.E. London, 8.4.23, C.Z.A., S6/272.

[47] Kisch to Stein, 27.4.23, C.Z.A., Z4/16085.

[48] See note 40 above; also Finkelstein to P.Z.E. Imm. Dept. 4.5.22, C.Z.A., S6/271.

[49] See minutes of the P.Z.E., 12.6.23, C.Z.A., unclassified.

[50] P.Z.E. circular to the Palestine Offices, confidential, March 1923, 8.5.23, both in S6/267.

[51] Circular to Palestine Offices, 24.10.22, and March 1923, S6/267; P.Z.E., Minutes of meetings, 11.3.23, 10.5.23; C.Z.A., unclassified.

[52] Circular to Palestine Offices, secret, 16.11.22, C.Z.A., S6/267.

[53] Pick to Palestine Office, Warsaw, 23.1.23, ibid.

[54] Circular to the Palestine Offices, 8.5.23, C.Z.A. S6/267; ibid, 2.6.24, C.Z.A. S6/268.

[55] Circular to Palestine Office, 23.1.23, C.Z.A. S6/267.

[56] Kisch to the Political Secretary, Z.O., London, confidential, 5.10.23, C.Z.A., Z4/16085; during May-November 1923, 2,883 Jews emigrated from Palestine: 796 residents before July 1920, and 1,875 who subsequently entered Palestine, see memo on 'Emigration from Palestine', P.Z.E., Imm. Dept., 14.12.23, C.Z.A., S6/274.

[57] Shuckburgh, minutes dated 1.10.23, C.O.733/48, file 45179.

[58] Cowen's report to the Z.E., see Z.E. meeting, 9.10.23, C.Z.A., Z4/302/9.

[59] Stein to Kisch, 12.11.23, C.Z.A. Z4/302/9.

[60] Ibid, ibid.

[61] See note 57 above.

[62] Z.E. Minutes of Meeting, 11.10.23, C.Z.A. Z4/302/8.

[63] Z.E. Minutes of Meeting, 16.10.23, ibid.

[64] P.Z.E. Minutes of Meeting, 12.10.23, C.Z.A.

[65] P.Z.E. Minutes of Meeting, 14.10.23, C.Z.A.

[66] 1,500 certificates for the half yearly Schedule, April-October 1925, and 7,500 for November 1925-March 1926. See Minutes of Palestine Executive Council, 1.5.25, 9.6.25, 14.10.25, all in C.O. 814/21.

[67] P.Z.E. Minutes of Meeting, 28.5.24, C.Z.A.

[68] Ibid, 18.6.24; Kisch, *Palestine Diary,* p. 130.

[69] P.Z.E. Minutes of Meetings, 17.2.25, 3.3.25, 18.3.25, 1.5.25, 3.5.25, 15.7.25, 19.7.25, C.Z.A.

[70] P.Z.E. Minutes of Meeting, 3.12.25, ibid.

[71] Ibid, 22.12.25.

[72] Ibid, 13.2.25.

[73] During 1926, 9,426 emigrated from Palestine, 7,365 of whom were Jews: 416 residents before July 1920 and 6,952 who entered the country

subsequently. *Palestine Administration Report,* 1926.

[74] P.Z.E. Minutes of meeting, 28.8.26, C.Z.A.

[75] See J. Gordon's (Acting Director, Zionist Immigration Department) report to P.Z.E., meeting, 6.8.26, ibid.

[76] Kisch to Z.E., 22.1.23, C.Z.A., Z4/16085; circular to Palestine Offices, confidential, July 1923, S/267.

[77] Ibid, 20.5.23, ibid.

[78] See note 5 above.

[79] Wyndham Deedes for the H.C. to Churchill, confidential despatch, 10.3.22, C.O.733/19/file 13565.

[80] See Public Notice, 1.8.21, note 10 above.

[81] Dennis M. Cohen for Director, Immigration Department, to District Governors, 13.3.22, I.S.A. 11/4.

[82] Morris to District Governor, 8.5.22, ibid.

[83] See pp. 120-21 above.

[84] Deedes, Acting H.C. to Churchill, confidential despatch, 11.5.22, C.O.733/21 file 24592.

[85] Kisch to Z.E., 22.1.23, C.Z.A. Z4/16085; Morris's confidential memo regarding irregularities, 12.10.23, C.O.733/50 file 51392.

[86] Van Vriesland to Chief Secretary, 21.9.22, C.Z.A., L3/31; P.Z.E. 'Memorandum on Immigration' 21.9.22, I.S.A. 11/6.

[87] See minutes of Conference on Immigration, 21.2.23, C.O.733/54 file 9748; S. Finkelstein, Z.O. London, to P.Z.E., 27.2.23, C.Z.A., S6/272.

[88] 351 single girls as compared with 65 married, P.Z.E. Immigration Department, Short Report and Budget proposal, 8.7.24, C.Z.A. S6/268.

[89] Hyamson in memo to Chief Secretary, 12.4.29, I.S.A. 11/4/12.

[90] Hyamson to C. Lambert, Immigration Officer, Jerusalem, 24.4.24, ibid.

[91] N. Mindel for Acting Director, Immigration Department, to Attorney General, 25.11.23, ibid.

[92] Attorney General to Director of Immigration, 26.11.23, ibid.

[93] See note 89 above.

[94] Attorney General to Director of Immigration, 8.2.24., I.S.A. 11/4/12.

[95] Hyamson to District Governors, 24.4.24, ibid.

[96] Hyamson to Cartwright, Immigration Officer, Warsaw, 10.6.24, I.S.A. 11/4.

[97] See note 89 above.

[98] Hyamson to District Commissioners, 27.8.25, I.S.A. 11/4/12.

[99] See note 89 above.

[100] H. Sacher, P.Z.E. to Chief Secretary, 18.3.29, 11/4/12.

[101] 1,500 skilled and unskilled women for April-September 1925 and 2,500 for October 1925-March 1926, see minutes of Palestine Executive Council, 1.5.25, and 14.10.25, respectively, C.O. 814/21.

[102] P.Z.E. Minutes of Meetings, 3.12.25, 22.12.25, C.Z.A.

[103] Ibid, 13.2.26.

[104] Ibid, 3.12.25.

[105] See pp. 126-7 above.

[106] P.Z.E. Minutes of meeting, 22.12.25, C.Z.A.

[107] During 1920-1923 — 10%, 1924-1931 — 21%, Giladi, p. 28.

[108] 1,815 out of 9,899, Palestine Administration Report, July 1920-June 1921.

[109] See p. 118 above.

[110] See Lichtheim, Zionist Office Berlin, to S. Finkelstein Z.O., London, 15.6.22, C.Z.A. Z4/1443.

[111] See Note 12 above.

[112] See Chapter 6 above, pp. 96-7.

[113] See note 19 above, also Eder to Morris 20.7.22, I.S.A. 11/4/2/1.

[114] Morris to Eder, 28.7.22, ibid.

[115] Only 76 immigrants during these three years.

[116] Hyamson to Cartwright, Imm. Office, Warsaw, 20.11.24, I.S.A., 11/4/2/1; Hyamson to P.Z.E., 29.5.25.

[117] See Note 54 above.

[118] P.Z.E. Memorandum on Immigration, 21.9.22, I.S.A. 11/6.

[119] See Chapter 6 above, pp. 107-8.

[120] Eder to Morris, 20.7.22; Morris to Eder 26.7.22; both in I.S.A. 11/4/2/2.

[121] Director, Commerce and Industry to Kisch, 11.1.23, C.Z.A., S6/274.

[122] Pick, in draft memorandum regarding middle class immigration, undated, S6/276.

[123] D. Giladi, *The Yishuv during 1924-1929: Economic and Political Aspects,* p. 31.

[124] Ibid, p. 34.

[125] Shuckburgh, memorandum to Secretary of State, 25.5.25, C.O.733/110 file 24403.

[126] Ibid., Shuckburgh wrote this memorandum following conversations with Hyamson and other Palestine officials while accompanying the Secretary of State on his visit to Palestine in April 1925.

[127] Hyamson in a memorandum to the Chief Secretary, 22.12.25, I.S.A., 11/4/2/6.

[128] See minutes of joint meeting of representatives of Palestine Offices abroad, with Hyamson, April 1925, I.S.A. 11/2/6.

[129] S. Moody, for Acting Chief Secretary in reply to Hyamson, 27.7.25, I.S.A. 11/1/1.

[130] Weizmann to Alfred Mond, 15.6.25, W.A.

[131] See Weizmann's report, minutes of Z.E. meeting, 3.7.25, C.Z.A., Z4/302/12.

[132] Kisch's report to the Zionist Executive regarding his interview with Ormsby Gore and Major Young, minutes of Z.E. meeting, 23.7.25, ibid.

[133] Shuckburgh to Weizmann in a reminder, 13.1.26, and Stein's replies, 15.1.25, 21.1.26, all in C.O.733/110 file 24403.

[134] See minutes of the Conference, 14.9.25, I.S.A. 11/1/5; also Kisch's notes in his *Diary,* p. 24.

[135] Hyamson to Chief Secretary, 11.5.26, I.S.A., 11/1/1/A.

[136] See the proposed Instruction enclosed in Plumer's confidential despatch to Amery, 8.4.26, C.O.733/111 file 1519.

[137] Weizmann to Kisch, 12.10.25, C.Z.A. Z4/16110.

[138] Kisch to Weizmann, 23.10.25, ibid., also Kisch's *Diary* pp. 211-12.
[139] Ibid, p. 212.
[140] See all the correspondence regarding the reorganisation of the Permit Section in C.O.733/112 file C4955 and C.O.733/117 file C20839.
[141] 1,085 in July, compared with 1,437 in May and 1,608 in June.
[142] See note 127 above.
[143] Stein to Shuckburgh 23.12.25, C.O.733/107 file 58037.
[144] See 'extracts from a letter from the Warsaw Palestine Office', 4.12.25, enclosed in Stein to Shuckburgh, ibid.
[145] See 'Observations of the Palestine Zionist Executive on the Immigration Ordinance', 17.5.26, C.O.733/116 file C17954.

CONCLUSION

The most commonly accepted view of immigration policy conceives it as primarily politically based and disregards, or at least underestimates, economic, psychological and bureaucratic factors, which significantly influenced both the policy and the extent of immigration. According to this version, the Zionists constantly pressed for large-scale immigration, while the Arabs demanded its complete suspension and the British reacted in accordance with these pressures. This rather schematic description, insofar as it broadly fits the circumstances of the 1930s and 1940s, does not accurately reflect the situation in Palestine during the five years of Sir Herbert Samuel's rule.

Herbert Samuel, the British statesman who played a major role in Zionist activity in London during World War I and subsequently became senior adviser of the Zionist Organisation on economic and political matters, was appointed to the post of High Commissioner in Palestine by virtue of British and Zionist confidence. His leading principle in the establishment of the Jewish National Home was, as he termed it himself, 'gradualist'. As far as it concerned Jewish immigration, this principle did not intend to limit immigration numerically, but to adjust its extent and economic structure to the absorptive capacity of the country. In practical terms, this meant that immigrants would be able to find employment upon their arrival and become integrated economically, without becoming a burden on the Administration.

Samuel did not change his approach as a result of the May Disturbances. However, during his first year in Palestine, he became less confident in the Zionists' ability to encourage middle-class immigration in possession of private capital and mobilize sufficient funds for the satisfactory absorption of labour immigration. Once convinced that the Zionists had failed to carry out these tasks successfully, Samuel came to the conclusion that it was necessary to reduce their power to select and regulate immigration and transfer control to the British authorities. From this point of view, the May Disturbances, although they added a certain dramatic dimension to the revision of policy, merely served to accelerate an unavoidable decision which Samuel would have reached sooner or later.

The principle of Economic Absorptive Capacity included in the White Paper of June 1922, gave official approval to a policy which had been in force since the beginning of the Civil Administration. Although the announcement of this principle affected Zionist prestige to a certain extent, it did not necessarily intend to restrict their activities in Palestine. This was proven during Samuel's last year in Palestine when, as a consequence of an unprecedented flow of middle-class immigration and capital into the country, labour immigration was considerably increased.

Samuel's sensitivity to the controversial nature of the immigration question and its political implications caused him to play it down as far as possible and to ensure that the making of policy would remain exclusively in his hands. This was shown by the limited powers granted to the Immigration Department and his avoidance of consultation with representatives of the population on matters regarding immigration. The lesson of the May Disturbances and Arab pressure to participate in control of immigration caused Samuel to change his former stand and propose setting up representative bodies, which would be authorised to discuss immigration questions. Yet, the proposed powers given to these bodies could not determine the policy nor the extent of immigration. On this issue, both Samuel and the Colonial Office were firm in their opinion that the only relevant principle to influence the policy should be economic and not political.

However, the implementation of the policy was a question of interpretation and execution by the machinery of control. In this matter there was a radical change after May 1921. The new Immigration Regulations of August 1921, the classification of immigrants and the inauguration of the Schedule System from July 1922 onwards, caused considerable bureaucratic difficulties to prospective immigrants and delays in receiving Immigration Certificates and visas, which inevitably reduced immigration. It seems that Samuel was not seriously concerned with the bureaucratic difficulties or with their effect on restriction of immigration. On this matter, he was drawn into conflict not only with the Zionists, but also with Major Morris, the Director of Immigration, whose task was to implement the policy. Samuel's disagreement with Morris was not over the necessity to make control stricter and more efficient, on which point they both agreed, but on how to reorganise the machinery of control: whether by Palestine Immigration Officers situated in the main centres of immigration, which would facilitate a smooth stream of immigration, as Morris suggested; or to leave the job for the British Consuls who would be instructed to refer every case to Jerusalem (Samuel's suggestion), a system which was liable to cause long delays and red tape.

The Zionist approach to the question of Jewish immigration during the period concerned was much more complicated and inconsistent than that of the British. The principal problem of the Zionists was their inability to make use of the opportunity placed at their disposal as a consequence of the Balfour Declaration, the San Remo Resolution and the appointment of Herbert Samuel as High Commissioner to Palestine. Their financial distress brought them, shortly after the setting up of the Civil Administration, to a humiliating position in which they were forced to ask the British to tighten control and restrict immigration. However, one year later, when Samuel inaugurated the new schemes of control, which intended to achieve the same aims, he was confronted with strong Zionist opposition. In this connection, Samuel wrote to Weizmann, in January 1922, 'if I had not enforced fairly close restrictions on immigration during the last few months and incurred a good deal of censure from the Zionist world for doing so, the Zionist Organisation would have had to act in the same direction, and borne the odium itself. I hope you will appreciate my friendly service!'[1]

The leading principle of the Zionist immigration policy was the principle of selection and regulation. On this issue the Zionists were in agreement with the British in their objection to 'free immigration', particularly during the early stages of the building up of the Jewish National Home, since in their opinion, immigration had to be selected 'so as to ensure the maximum and the most productive contribution to the structure'.[2] The difference of opinion between the British and the Zionists was on the question of who would do the selecting and regulating. However, even on this issue, the Zionists were not unified. The question was whether to ask for full control over immigration, or to ask only for closest co-operation while the final decision would be left to the British. This latter approach, which was supported by Weizmann, could ensure a convenient position for the Zionist leadership within the Movement, reduce criticism from their own people, conceal their financial difficulties and place responsibility for the restricted policy on the British. Nevertheless, the Zionists were firm and consistent in their demands that primary control and selection of immigration should be left to their own discretion. On this issue, Weizmann succeeded in obtaining British agreement to his stand. His success was due to his ability to pinpoint the main British fear — the danger of infiltration to Palestine by politically undesirable elements who could cause agitation and unrest — and to offer the Zionists help in this task.

The attitude of the Palestinian Arabs towards the question of immigration was plain, consistent and extremist. Their uncompromising demand for total suspension of all Jewish immigration left very little room for manoeuvre to both the British and the Zionists. Their unconditional rejection of the British proposals to set up representative bodies which could give them, if not control, a certain influence over the policy, closed for them the door to even token participation in the making of policy.

Considering the political dependence of the Zionists on the British and their limited economic ability to absorb large scale immigration during the period concerned, it might have been possible to reach an Arab-Zionist agreement regarding the policy and the extent of immigration which may have satisfied the Arabs. Yet, the Arab rejection of such an agreement gave the Administration a free hand over control, which made possible the flow of immigration during 1924-1925.

NOTES

[1] Samuel to Weizmann, 20.1.22, C.Z.A., Z4/16146.
[2] Kisch's notes in his *Diary* p. 130; in P.Z.E. meeting 18.6.24, see p. 130 above.

Appendix 1

IMMIGRATION ORDINANCE, 1920*

WHEREAS it is necessary to make provision for regulating the entry into Palestine of persons desiring to reside there permanently or temporarily.

IT IS HEREBY ORDERED AS FOLLOWS:—

1. Entry into Palestine, either for permanent or temporary residence, shall be regulated by the High Commissioner from time to time according to the conditions and needs of the country.

2. The High Commissioner may appoint a Director of Immigration and other Immigration Officers to control the entry of all persons into Palestine. The Director and the officers so appointed shall have the power to enter on board any vessel or railway train, to detain or examine any person desiring to enter Palestine, and to require the production from such person of any letters, written messages or memoranda, or any written or printed matter, including plans, photographs, and other pictorial representations.

3. Every person who desires to enter Palestine, whether by sea or land or air, must be in possession of a passport or other permit or papers of identity. The photograph of the holder, save in the case of Moslem women, shall be attached to the passport or permit or papers.

4. Every person resident in Palestine at the date of this Ordinance who leaves the country and intends to return shall obtain in accordance with the Palestine Passport Regulations a passport of Laissez-Passer which he shall produce on demand to the Immigration Officer.

---

* *Official Gazette of the Government of Palestine,* No. 27, 16 September 1920.

157

5.   No person shall enter Palestine except with the leave of the Director of Immigration, or an Immigration Officer duly authorised by him, unless he has been permanently resident in Palestine since the British Occupation or was so resident within a year of the outbreak of war. The Director of Immigration shall refuse leave, unless the person satisfies the following conditions:—

(a) That he is in possession of a passport or permit endorsed or *visé* at a British Passport Office or by a British Consul or other official authorised to grant *visa* or permits on behalf of H.M. Government.

(b) That he has in his possession or is in a position to obtain the means of supporting himself and any dependants who desire to enter with him.

(c) That he is not a lunatic, idiot, or me[n]tally deficient.

(d) That he is not the subject of a certificate given by a Medical Inspector that on medical grounds to be specified by order from time to time he should not be permitted to land.

(e) That he has not been sentenced in a foreign country for any crime for which extradition may be granted.

(f) That he has not been prohibited from entering the country by the High Commissioner.

(g) That he fulfils such other requirements as may be prescribed by any general or special instructions of the Director of Immigration.

(h) Such fee shall be payable by an immigrant on admission as may be determined by the High Commissioner by the regulation.

6.   (a) An Immigration Officer or a Medical Inspector may inspect any person seeking to enter Palestine and may detain him provisionally.

(b) Where leave to enter is refused, the person may be temporarily detained in such manner as the High Commissioner may direct at some place and while so detained shall be deemed to be in legal custody.

(c) The Director of Immigration or an Immigration Officer duly authorised by him may order that a person arriving on a ship to whom leave to enter is refused shall be removed from Palestine by the Master of the ship on which he arrived or by the owners or agents of that ship, to the country of which he is a national or from which he embarked for Palestine.

7. Any person allowed to enter shall within 15 days of his arrival in Palestine register at the Police Headquarters of the District in which he resides the particulars set out in the schedule hereto.

This provision shall not apply to persons certified by the Consular *visé* to be travellers, or persons in transit to another country, whose stay in Palestine will not exceed three months from the date of entry. In case any person so certified overstays the period he shall register immediately at the place in which he is resident and shall apply to the Director of Immigration for a permit to stay for a further period in Palestine.

8. The High Commissioner may make an order in either of the following cases for the deportation, within five years of his entry into Palestine, of any person who has not become a citizen of Palestine, and may by such order require such person to leave and to remain thereafter out of Palestine:—

(a) If any court certifies that he has been sentenced to a term of imprisonment exceeding one month for an offence under this Ordinance or otherwise, and recommends that an order for deportation should be made in his case.

(b) If any Court certifies within one year of his last entry into Palestine that he has been found wandering without ostensible means of subsistance, or has been sentenced in a foreign country for a crime for which he is liable to be extradited.

(c) If the High Commissioner deems it to be conducive to the public good to make such an order.

A person against whom such an order is made may be expelled from Palestine and sent to the country of which he is a national. The order may extend to the dependants of such person.

The High Commissioner may apply any money or property of such person in payment of the expenses of his journey and the maintenance, until his departure, of himself and his dependants.

An order made under this article may be subject to any condition which the High Commissioner may think proper. A person with respect to whom a deportation order has been made shall leave Palestine in accordance with the order, and shall thereafter so long as the order is in force remain out of **Palestine.**

9.   If any person acts in contravention of or fails to comply with any of the provisions of this Ordinance or any order or rule made thereunder, or aids or abets in any such contravention, or harbours any person whom he knows or has reasonable ground for believing to have acted in contravention of [t]his Ordinance, he shall be guilty of an offence against this Ordinance. Any person shall be guilty of an offence if he:

(a) Refuses to answer any question reasonably put to him by the Director of Immigration of any official acting under his orders or to produce any document in his possession.

(b) Makes any false return or false statement.

(c) Alters any certificate or copy of a certificate or any entry made in pursuance of this Ordinance.

(d) Obstructs or impedes an official in the exercise of his duties.

(e) Without lawful authority uses or has in his possession any forged, altered, or irregular passport or permit or other document, or any passport or document on which any *visa* or endorsement has been altered or forged.

(f) Remains in Palestine after an order for his deportation has been notified to him.

Any person found guilty of a contravention will be liable to a fine not exceeding £E.100 or to imprisonment for a term [not] exceeding 6 months, without prejudice to any prosecution to which he may be liable under any other law.

10.   The High Commissioner may direct that any person or class of persons shall be exempted wholly or in part, and either unconditionally or subject to such conditions as he may impose, from the provisions of this Ordinance.

Nothing in this Ordinance shall apply to

(a) Any duly accredited head of a foreign diplomatic mission or any member of his household or of his official staff, or to any duly accredited Consul de Carriere.

(b) Any member of the British Military, Naval, and Air Forces in uniform and any member of the Civil Government entering or leaving Palestine on duty.

11.   The Director of Immigration may with the approval of the High Commissioner issue from time to time any orders or

regulations for the better control of immigration into Palestine.

12.　　　This Ordinance shall be known as the Immigration Ordinance 1920 and shall come into force from 1st September.

Herbert Samuel
High Commissioner
for Palestine.

Government House
Palestine. 26th August
　　　　1920.
　　Ref. 7961/Q.

Appendix 2

INSTRUCTIONS TO CONSULS REGARDING
GRANTING OF VISAS FOR PALESTINE*

With reference to Section XIV. of the General Instructions, the provisions contained herein will henceforth regulate the granting of visas for Palestine, and all previous instructions regarding immigration into that country, including instructions issued by the Foreign Office, are hereby cancelled.

1. Cancellation of previous instructions.

The Palestine Administration will issue an Immigration Ordinance establishing a general control over immigration. The Palestine Ordinance will be similar in form to the Aliens Order, 1920, which is applicable to the United Kingdom. A copy of the Palestine Ordinance will be sent to you as soon as possible, and you should pay special attention to this in order that the granting of visas may conform to the immigration regulations.

2. Palestine Immigration Ordinance.

In order to proceed with the establishment of the Jewish National Home in Palestine, the Palestine Administration will act in co-operation with the Zionist Organisation. The Palestine Administration will fix the total number and class of Zionists for whom employment and accommodation can be provided over a given period, say one year. The Central Zionist Organisation will fix the proportion who are to proceed from each country, and will

3. Establishment of Jewish National Home.

* F.O. 371/5184 file E9523/476/44

162

inform their various branches. You will be authorised either direct by this Department, or through His Majesty's Representative locally, of the total number and class of Zionists to whom you may grant visas for Palestine during the period in question. You should then grant visas accordingly to these who are recommended to you by the local branch of the Zionist Organisation, unless you definitely consider that any particular individual so recommended to you is undesirable. You should distribute the number of visas granted as far as possible equally over the particular period, but generally you should act in co-operation with the local branch of the Zionist Organisation.

4. Zionists may be accompanied by their families.

A Zionist who has been granted a visa under Section 3 hereof may be accompanied by his family, and for this purpose the members of his family shall be deemed to consist of his wife, children, and persons wholly dependent on him, but a separate permit should be required for all males over 16 years of age. Visas may therefore be granted to the members of the family, but in calculating the total number to whom you are authorised to grant visas under Section 3, the members of the family shall not be taken into account.

5. Persons other than Zionists.

In addition to Zionists recommended by the Zionist Organisation as above, visas for Palestine may be granted to the following classes, irrespective of creed or nationality.
  (a) Any person who can satisfy you that he is self-supporting or can produce evidence that he can obtain employment in Palestine.
  (b) Persons of religious occupation, including the class of Jews who have gone to Palestine in recent years through religious motives, and who can satisfy you that they will have means of maintenance there.

(c) Persons in Government services.
(d) Members of families of present residents in Palestine.

**6.
Ex-enemy
aliens.**

Ex-enemy aliens are not to be treated on a different footing from other persons, and they may therefore be granted visas for Palestine provided they fall within any of the classes of persons to whom you are authorised to grant visas under these regulations, and you have no definite reason for regarding any particular individual as undesirable.

**7.
Special care in
granting visas.**

You should exercise special care in granting visas for Palestine, and satisfy yourself that there is no known objection to the persons to whom you grant facilities.

FOREIGN OFFICE,
20th August, 1920.

Appendix 3

PUBLIC NOTICE

Admission of Immigrants into Palestine*

New regulations have now been drawn up governing the admission of immigrants into Palestine. Apart from Travellers, that is to say, persons who do not intend to remain in Palestine more than three months, and returning residents. Immigrants into Palestine are divided into the five undermentioned categories:—

'B' (1) Persons of independent means who intend to take up permanent residence in Palestine.

'C' (2) Members of professions who intend to follow their calling.

'D' (3) Wives, children and other persons wholly dependent on residents of Palestine.

'E' (4) Persons who have a definite prospect of employment with specified employers or enterprises.

'F' (5) Persons of religious occupations, including the class of Jews who have come to Palestine in recent years from religious motives and who can show that they have means of maintenance here.

A person who desires to settle in Palestine must obtain a visa from a British Consul or other British Passport Control Officer whom he will have to satisfy that he belongs to one of the above-mentioned categories.

Members of professions will have to produce their diplomas or other indubitable evidence of qualification in their professions.

Wives, children and other persons wholly dependent on residents in Palestine will be required to produce evidence that their relatives in Palestine are both willing and in a position to support them.

The quickest and most satisfactory method is for the relative in Palestine to apply to the Governor of the district in which he lives either direct or through some person or organisation of a

* Official Gazette of the Government of Palestine, 15 August 1921.

165

representative character for a certificate in the following terms:—
'I (AB) hereby certify that (the prospective immigrant) is the wife, child, etc. of (the resident in Palestine) who is both willing and in a position to support him (her).' This certificate when completed and signed should be sent to the prospective immigrant with instructions to take it to the nearest British Consul or Passport Control Officer in support of his request for a visa for Palestine.

Much time will also be saved if persons who wish to introduce immigrants belonging to category 4 into Palestine will communicate in the first place with the Department of Immigration & Travel, Jerusalem, stating the name and present address of the prospective immigrant, the nature of the employment offered to him, and the name and address of the prospective employer.

　　　　　　　　　　　　　ALBERT M. HYAMSON
1 August, 1921.　　　　　Immigration & Travel.

Appendix 4

IMMIGRATION ORDINANCE, 1925*
ARTICLE 2

(2) No person shall be granted an immigration certificate unless he belongs to one of the following categories:— *Categories of Immigrants.*

(A) Persons of independent means, which term shall be deemed to include: *Category A.*

(i) Any person who is in *bona fide* possession, and freely disposes, of a capital of not less than £E.500, and is qualified in a profession or intends to engage in commerce or agriculture: and

(ii) Any person who is in *bona fide* possession, and freely disposes, of a capital of not less than £E.250 and is skilled in a trade or craft; and

(iii) Any person who has a secure income of not less than £E.60 per annum, exclusive of earned income; and

(iv) Any orphan of less than 16 years of age whose maintenance is assured until such time as he is able to support himself; and

(v) Any person of religious occupation whose maintenance is assured; and

(vi) Any student whose maintenance is assured until such time as he is able to support himself.

---

* GOVERNMENT OF PALESTINE, *ORDINANCES 1925*.

(B) Persons who are not in *bona fide* possession, or do not freely dispose, of a capital of the full amount of £E.500, but would otherwise have belonged to Category A (i).   *Category B.*

(C) Persons who have a definite prospect of employment in Palestine.   *Category C.*

(D) Dependants of permanent residents or of immigrants belonging to Categories A, B and C other than Categories A (iv) and (vi):   *Category D.*

Provided that an immigration certificate may be granted by the Chief Immigration Officer, at his discretion, to any near relative of a permanent resident who is wholly and directly dependent upon such permanent resident, notwithstanding that he may not fall within the delinition of 'Dependant' in the Ordinance.

Appendix 5

JEWISH IMMIGRATION INTO PALESTINE
JULY 1920 — APRIL 1921*

Month	With Z.C. Guarantee	Without Z.C. Guarantee	Total
July 1920	413	—	413
August	1105	—	1105
September	1503	—	1503
October	674	116	790
November	1166	18	1184
December	1135	307	1442
January 1921	524	182	706
February	463	178	641
March	1061	188	1249
April	1145	472	1619
TOTAL	9191	1461	10652

---

* Based on Samuel's reports to Foreign Office and Colonial Office and on Zionist sources, Z/4 1269.

Appendix 6

JEWISH IMMIGRATION INTO PALESTINE 1919-1928 MONTHLY TREND*

II. P.Z.E. Records of Jewish Immigration Table No. 6 Monthly Trend of Immigration

	1919	1920	1921	1922	1923	1924	1925	1926	1927	1928
January	—	332	576	940	890	350	1604	1565	102	75
February	—	182	509	933	834	318	1732	1428	134	44
March	—	273	763	730	808	439	3018	2235	299	45
April	—	255	1277	826	866	790	2460	1447	274	45
May	—	171	291	802	844	572	2715	1492	284	103
June	—	434	155	530	835	1336	3694	1308	286	50
July	—	689	446	434	485	1317	2528	707	225	35
August	—	1145	615	571	646	1888	3167	782	107	87
September	23	1790	899	494	572	2026	3269	654	191	71
October	74	583	806	611	477	835	3684	666	118	64
November	51	1154	817	1042	487	1533	2644	499	182	64
December	653	1215	1140	772	349	1501	2620	461	118	99
Total	806	8223	8294	8685	8093	12905	33135	13244	2320	784
Tourists remaining in Palestine	—	—	—	—	82	987	1251	611	714	1287
Grand Total	806	8223	8294	8685	8175	13892	34386	13855	3034	2071

* PALESTINE ZIONIST EXECUTIVE, IMMIGRATION DEPARTMENT, TEN YEARS OF JEWISH IMMIGRATION INTO PALESTINE, 1919-1928

Appendix 7
JEWISH IMMIGRATION INTO PALESTINE 1919-1928 DISTRIBUTION BY CATEGORIES†

II. P.Z.E. Records of Jewish Immigration Table No. 7 Distribution by Categories

Year	Capitalists Men	Capitalists Women	Capitalists Children	Dependents upon Residents of Palestine Men	Dep. Women	Dep. Children	Labour Men	Labour Women	Labour Dependents Men	Lab. Dep. Women	Lab. Dep. Children	Others, without categories & unknown* Men	Others Women	Others Children	Total Men	Total Women	Total Children	Unknown	Total	Tourists remaining	Grand total
1919	—	—	—	—	—	—	—	—	—	—	—	329	263	214	329	263	214		806		806
1920	—	—	—	—	—	—	—	—	—	—	—	4325	1348	971	4325	1348	971	1579	8223	—	8223
1921	—	—	—	—	—	—	—	—	—	—	—	4542	1732	1335	4542	1732	1335	685	8294		8294
1922	255	156	125	732	1121	725	913	151	18	157	230	1575	852	849	3493	2437	1929	826	8685		8685
1923	241	162	157	457	987	569	1916	286	135	821	995	12	9	4	2761	2265	1725	1342	8093	82	8175
1924	1392	1256	1605	379	1152	715	2634	550	10	718	1111	459	380	544	4874	4056	3975		12905	987	13892
1925	3583	3234	3400	1187	3009	1465	8244	2639	34	2175	2901	455	331	478	13503	11388	8244		33135	1251	34386
1926	528	422	375	374	1088	660	4577	1860	36	992	1313	352	295	372	5867	4657	2720		13244	611	13855
1927	86	70	42	149	415	300	316	300	1	77	94	158	123	189	710	985	625		2320	714	3034
1928	68	44	53	53	212	154	107	53	1	19	17	—	—	—	232	328	224		784	1287	2071
Total	6153	5344	5757	3334	7984	4588	18707	5839	235	4959	6661	12207	5333	4956	40636	29459	21962	4432	96489	4932	101421
Subtotal	17254			15906			24546		11855			22496			92057						
Percent	6.1	5.3	5.6	3.3	7.9	4.5	18.5	5.7	0.2	4.9	6.6	12.0	5.3	4.9	40.1	29.1	21.6	4.4	95.2	4.8	100
Percent (subtotal)	17.0			15.7			24.2		11.7			22.2			90.8						

*There was no classification by categories prior to 1922

†PALESTINE ZIONIST EXECUTIVE IMMIGRATION DEPARTMENT
TEN YEARS OF JEWISH IMMIGRATION INTO PALESTINE 1919-1928

BIBLIOGRAPHY

I Unpublished Sources

A. ARCHIVES

1. *Public Record Office, London (P.R.O.)*
   C.O. 733   — Colonial Office, Palestine
   C.O. 537   — Colonial Office, Palestine, Supplementary Papers
   C.O. 814   — Colonial Office, Palestine, Sessional Papers
   F.O. 371   — Foreign Office, General Correspondence, Political
   F.O. 372   — Foreign Office, General Correspondence, Non-Political
   F.O. 406   — Foreign Office, Confidential Prints
   CAB.   — Cabinet Papers

2. *Israel State Archives, Jerusalem (I.S.A.)*
   2   — Chief Secretary, Palestine Government
   11   — Department of Immigration and Travel, Palestine Government

3. *Central Zionist Archives, Jerusalem (C.Z.A.)*
   Z4   — Zionist Organisation, Central Office, London
   Z4/302   — Zionist Executive, London, Minutes of meetings
   L3   — Zionist Commission, Jerusalem
   L4   — Zionist Commission, Jaffa
   S6   — Palestine Zionist Executive, Immigration Department
   S25   — Palestine Zionist Executive, Political Department
   Unclassified   — Palestine Zionist Executive, Minutes of meetings.
   J1   — Va'ad Leumi, (Jewish National Council)

4. *Weizmann Archives, Rehovot (W.A.)*
   W.A.   — chronologically arranged

B Ph.D. DISSERTATIONS

Caplan, Neil, 'The Yishuv and the Arab Question, 1917-1925', University of London, 1973.

Friesel, Avyatar, 'Weizmann's First Steps in the Leadership of the Zionist Movement, 1917-1921,' (Hebrew), Hebrew University, Jerusalem, 1970.

Giladi, Dan, 'The Yishuv during the Fourth Aliyah, 1924-1929, Economic and Political Examination,' Hebrew University, Jerusalem, 1968 (Hebrew).

172

Gil-Har, Yitzhak, 'The Organisation and Self-Government of the Yishuv in Palestine, 1917-1922,' Hebrew University, 1972, (Hebrew).

Mandel, Neville, 'Turks, Arabs and Jewish Immigration into Palestine, 1882-1914,' Oxford, 1965.

II Published Sources

A BRITISH OFFICIAL PUBLICATIONS

1. *Command Papers:* (in chronological order)

Mandates, *Final Draft of the Mandates for Mesopotamia and Palestine,* Cmd. 1500, London 1921.

Palestine, *Disturbances in May 1921: Reports of the Commission of Inquiry with Correspondence Relating Thereto,* Cmd. 1540, October 1921 (Haycraft Report).

Palestine, *Correspondence with the Palestine Arab Delegation and the Zionist Organisation,* Cmd. 1700, June 1922 (Churchill's White Paper).

Palestine, *Papers Relating to the Elections for the Palestine Legislative Council, 1923,* Cmd. 1889, June 1923.

Palestine, *Proposed Formation of an Arab Agency: Correspondence with the High Commissioner for Palestine,* Cmd. 1989, November 1923.

Palestine Royal Commission, Report, Cmd. 5479, July 1937 (Peel Report)

2. *Reports*

Palestine and Trans-Jordan, Report to the Council of the League of Nations, on the Administration of — 1920/1, 1922, 1923, 1924, 1925, 1926 (title varies), London.

Palestine, *Report of the High Commissioner on the Administration of Palestine, 1920-1925,* London, 1925 (Samuel, Report).

3. *Other*

Documents on British Foreign Policy, First Series, vol. IV, ed. E. L. Woodward and R. Butler, London 1952.

Documents on British Foreign Policy, First Series, vol. XIII, ed. R. Butler and J. P. T. Bury, London 1963.

Palestine, Government of, *Ordinances,*

Palestine, Government of, *Quarterly List of Senior Officials.*

Palestine, Government of, *Staff List.*

Palestine, Government of, *Official Gazette,* July 1920-December 1926.

B   ZIONIST OFFICIAL PUBLICATIONS

Political Report of the Executive . . . to the XIIth Zionist Congress, Carlsbad, September 1921, London 1921.

Report of the XIIth Zionist Congress, Carlsbad, September 1st-14th 1921; Addresses, Reports, Resolutions, London 1922.

The Mandate for Palestine, memo to the Council of the League of Nations, July 1922, London 1922.

Report of the Executive to the XIIIth Zionist Congress Carlsbad, August 1923, London 1923.

Report of the Executive of the Zionist Organisation submitted to the 14th Zionist Congress at Vienna, London 1925.

Resolutions of the 14th Zionist Congress, Vienna 1925, London 1925.

Resolutions of the 15th Zionist Congress, Basle 1927, London 1928.

C   LETTERS, DIARIES, MEMOIRS AND BIOGRAPHIES

Amery, Leopold Charles: *My Political Life,* Vol 2, London, 1953.

Ben Gurion, David: *Igrot* (Letters), ed. & annotated Y. Erez, Tel Aviv, 1972, vol. II — 1920-1928.

. . . *Zikhronot,* (Memoirs), Tel Aviv, 1971, (vol. I).
Bentwich, Norman and Michael Kisch, *Brigadier Frederick Kisch: Soldier and Zionist,* London, 1966.

Bowle, John: *Viscount Samuel,* London, 1957.

Frumkin, Gad, *Derekh Shofet bi-Irushalayim* (The Way of a Judge in Jerusalem), Tel Aviv, 1954.

Hobman, J.B. (ed): *David Eder: Memoirs of a Modern Pioneer,* London, 1945.

Katzenelson, Berl: *Igrot 1919-1922* (Letters) Tel Aviv, 1970.

. . . *Kitvai Berl Katzenelson* (Writings), Tel Aviv 1946 and 1950 (vols. I and II).

Kisch, Frederick H: *Palestine Diary,* London 1938.

Meinertzhagen, Richard: *Middle East Diary, 1917-1956,* London, 1959.

Nordau, Max: *Zikhronot (Memoirs), Tel Aviv, 1929.*

Ruppin, Arthur: *Memoirs, Diaries, Letters,* ed. A. Bein, London/Jerusalem, 1970.

. . . *Pirkai Hayay* (Chapters of my Life), ed. A. Bein, Tel Aviv, 1968 (vol. III).

Samuel, Edwin: *A Lifetime in Jerusalem,* Jerusalem, 1970.

Samuel, Herbert: *Memoirs,* London, 1945.

Sprinzak, Yosef: *Igrot* (Letters), Tel Aviv, 1965, (vol. I 1910-1929).

Storrs, Ronald: *Orientations,* definitive ed., London 1943.

Weizmann, Chaim, *Trial and Error,* London 1949.

D   GENERAL WORKS

Abcarius, M.F.: *Palestine through the Fog of Propaganda,* London, 1946.

Antonius, George: *The Arab Awakening,* London, 1938.

Assaf, Michael: *ha-Yihasim bein Aravim ve-Yehudim be-Eretz-Israel, 1860-1948,* (Arab-Jewish Relations in Palestine), Tel Aviv, 1970.

Attias, Moshe: ed., *Sefer Hateudot shel ha-Va'ad ha-Leumi le-Knesset Israel be-Eretz-Israel, 1918-1948,* (Documents of the V.L.), Jerusalem, 1963.

Bein, Alex: *The Return to the Soil,* Jerusalem, 1952.

Bentwich, Norman: *England in Palestine,* London 1932.

Breslavski, Moshe: *Tnuat ha-Poalim ha-Eretzyisraelit,* (The Eretz-Israel Labour Movement), Tel Aviv, 1966 (vol. II).

Cohen, Aharon: *Israel and the Arab World,* New York, 1970.

Dinur, B.Z. *et al:* see *Sefer Toldot Ha-Hagana.*

ESCO Foundation for Palestine, Inc., *Palestine: A Study of Jewish, Arab and British Policies,* New Haven, 1947 (vol. I).

Graves, Philip: *Palestine, The Land of Three Faiths,* London 1923.

Halpern, Ben: *The Idea of the Jewish State,* Cambridge, Mass. 1969.

Hanna, Paul Lamont: *British Policy in Palestine,* Washington, 1942.

Horowitz, David: *Hakalkalah ha-Artzi-Yisraelit be-Hitpatchutah,* (Palestine Economy in Development), Tel Aviv, 1944.

Hurewitz, J.C.: *Diplomacy in the Near and Middle East: A Documentary Record, 1914-1956,* Princeton, N.J., 1956, (vol. II).

Hyamson, Albert Montefiore: *Palestine, A Policy,* London, 1942.

. . . *Palestine Under the Mandate 1920-1948,* London, 1950.

Ingrams, Doreen: (ed.), *Palestine Papers 1917-1922: Seeds of Conflict,* London, 1972.

Jeffries, Joseph: *Palestine, The Reality,* London, 1929.

Kedourie, Elie: *The Chatham House Version and other Middle Eastern Studies,* Cass, London, 1970.

. . . *England and the Middle East: The Destruction of the Ottoman Empire,* London, 1956.

Klieman, Aaron S.: *Foundations of British Policy in the Arab World: The Cairo Conference of 1921,* Baltimore/London 1970.

Laqueur, Walter: *A History of Zionism,* London, 1972.

Medzini, Moshe: *Esser Shanim shel Mediniut Eretzyisraelit,* (Ten Years of Palestine Politics), Tel Aviv, 1928.

Marlowe, John: *Seat of Pilate,* London 1959.

Monroe, Elizabeth: *Britain's Moment in the Middle East 1914-1956,* London 1965.

Porath, Yehoshua: *The Emergence of the Palestinian Arab National Movement, 1918-1929,* Frank Cass, London, 1977.

Sefer ha-Teudot . . . see Attias.

Sefer Toldot ha-Hagana, (History of the Haganah), ed. B.Z. Dinur *et al.,* Tel Aviv, 1964, (vol. B. pt. 1).

Stein, Leonard: *The Balfour Declaration,* London 1961.

Sykes, Christopher: *Cross Roads to Israel: Palestine From Balfour to Bevin,* London 1967.

INDEX

Action Committee, 44
Admission Regulations (1921), text, 165-6
Advisory Council (Palestine), 7-8, 74
Allenby, Lord, 20, 23, 25, 27-8
American support, 9, 14, 42
Arab Agency, 74-6, 78
Arab Congress, Third (1920), 17-18
Arab Congress, Fifth (1922), 71-2
Arab Congress, Sixth (1923), 74
Arab Executive, 18-23, 73
Asquith, Herbert, 2, 3-4

Balfour, A.J., 43
Balfour Declaration, 3, 19, 37, 51, 52, 55-6, 59, 73
Bentwich, Norman, 6, 102, 108-109, 135
Bols, Maj.-Gen., 59
Bratislava, 11

Camps, Zionist Immigration, 126, 131
categories, for immigrants: defined, 38, 99, 165-6; revised, 112, 118-21, 139, 167-8
Certificate System, 84, 98, 103, 104, 143, 144
Churchill, Winston, 18, 25, 27, 40, 41, 43-5, 51-2, 60
Clauson, G.M., 50, 111, 118
Clayton, G., 74, 75
Cohen, Dennis, 8, 126
Colonial Office, 40-51, 84-5, 95-6, 111, 127-8
Communists, 19
Constantinople, 29-30, 86
Consuls, British, 11, 14, 84, 85, 113-14, 118

Cowen, Joseph, 23, 25, 128
Curzon, Lord, 1, 83

Deedes, Wyndham, 73, 105
Devonshire, Duke of, 90
Diaspora Jews, 66, 68, 71

Economic Absorptive Capacity, 56, 59, 60, 117-33, 153
Economy Committee (Jerusalem), 88
Eder, Dr. D., 6-7, 23-4, 57, 66, 67, 69-70
Egypt, resistance to immigrants, 27-8, 85

fees, as revenue, 85-7, 88
fiancées, admission of, 133-8
Finkelstein, S., 103
Forbes Adam, 100
Foreign Office, 6, 28, 83-6

guaranteed immigrants, 47-9, 51, 95

Haifa, 29
Halutzim (Jewish pioneers), 11, 44
Hapoel Hatzair, 66
Hyamson, Albert M., 8, 77, 82-3, 91-2, 105-106, 111, 113-14, 135-6, 141-4

Immigration and Travel Department, 7-8, 39, 77, 82-3, 86, 91-2
Immigration Board, proposed, 5, 57
Immigration Committee, 72-3, 76-7, 89, 107
Immigration Conference (1921), 84, 95, 121

Immigration Conference (1925), 143, 145
Immigration Inspectors (Officers), 28, 35-6, 49, 70, 83-5, 97, 99, 108
Immigration Ordinance (1920), 6-7, 109; text, 157-61
Immigration Ordinance (1925), 95-114, 143-5; text of Article 2, 167-8
Immigration Regulations (1921), 66-8, text, 165-6
immigration statistical tables, 169, 170, 171

Jaffa, 17, 19-25, 29
Jewish National Council, 24, 26
Jewish National Home, 1, 6, 27, 40, 52, 59, 66, 95, 152, 155

Kantara, 29
Keith-Roach, E., 111
Keren Hayesod, 42, 44
Keren Kayemet, 66
Kisch, Col. F., 105, 130, 131, 143, 144-5

Labour Pool, 69, 98, 102, 104, 105, 124-5
Labour Schedules, 95, 96, 104-106, 109-10, 121-7
Landman, Samuel, 25
Legislative Council, proposed, 72, 73, 76-7, 89
Lloyd George, D., 1, 43

Mandate, League of Nations, 1, 59-60, 75
May Day Disturbances (1921), 17-21, 153
Meinertzhagen, Col. R., 71
middle-class immigrants, 138-46
Mindel, N.I., 8, 28, 29, 111
Moody, S., 128
Morris, Maj., 8, 77, 88-9, 91, 154; European visits, 14, 28-31; Labour Pool, 69-70; in London, 45; revised scheme, 35, 36, 39, 101-102

Morris Report, 46-8
Musa Kazim, 52, 54-5, 75

non-guaranteed immigrants, 47-9, 50-51

Palestine Administration, 3, 59, 97, 98, 121, 134-5
Palestine Arab Delegation, 41-2, 51-60, 71-2; second visit, 74-5
Palestine Offices, see under Zionist Organisation
Palestine Zionist Executive, 65-9, 103-104, 110, 119, 126-31, 132-4, 136-8
Parkin, R.T., 12, 100
Pick, Prof., H., 66, 129, 131
Plumer, Lord, 142-3
Poland, 30-31, 140, 144, 145; see also Warsaw

Rabbinate, 24
Ruppin, Dr. A., 9, 66, 67, 68, 70, 128

Sacher, H., 68
Samuel, Sir H., 1-4, 142, 152-4; Administration reorganisation, 87-91; Advisory Council recommendation, 74; Colonial Office proposals, 45-6, 58, 96-8; early scheme, 9-11, 19-24, 40; Labour Schedule, 106-107; revised scheme, 35-40, 50, 66-9, 110; Statement of Policy, 37-40, 51, 96-7, 117
San Remo Peace Conference, 1, 3, 8
Shuckburgh, John, 48, 54-5, 128
skilled labour immigrants, 48, 51, 119, 123
Sokolow, Nahum, 4, 23, 26
Solomon, Col., 105
Spencer, Maj., 100
Sprinzak, J., 66, 67, 129, 131
Statement of British Policy, see White Paper (1922)
Stein, Leonard, 12, 49-50
Symes, 145

Tel Aviv, 141-2
Trieste, 29, 30, 85, 86

unemployment, 120, 124, 132, 134, 137
Ussishkin, Menachem, 66, 68

van Vriesland, Dr. S., 66, 130
Vienna, 30, 85, 86
visas, instructions to Consuls, 162-4

Warsaw, 85, 86, 127, 136, 146
Weizmann, Dr. Chaim, 3, 4, 5, 9, 26, 96, 104-105, 107, 125, 155; Arab Delegation, 54-5, 78; London visit, 42-50, 60, 78
White Paper (1922), 58-60, 71, 117

Young, Maj., 53, 100
Young-Batterbee Committee, 101

Zionist Commission, 6, 9-10, 24, 29, 36

Zionist Conference (1920), 9
Zionist Congress, Twelfth (1921), 65
Zionist Executive, 10-13, 126; Colonial Office negotiations, 41, 95-6, 101-104, 107; counter proposals, 98-100, 103-104, 107-108; draft ordinance comments, 112-113; Labour Schedule, 128, 134; reorganisation, 65-71, 126; restriction of immigration, 25-8, 44, 46-9; see also under Palestine Zionist Executive
Zionist Organisation, 3, 56, 60; Central Office, 12-13; control responsibility, 4, 36, 43-51, 95-101, 110; early schemes, 4-6, 11; financial difficulties, 12, 84-5; Palestine Offices, 70, 71, 84; policy review, 154-5; recommended immigrants, 11, 38-9, 49, 97-8
Zionist Orthodox Movement (Mizrachi), 66